ISBN 978-1-331-00722-7
PIBN 10132716

English
Français
Deutsche
Italiano
Español
Português

www.forgottenbooks.com

Mythology Photography **Fiction**
Fishing Christianity **Art** Cooking
Essays Buddhism Freemasonry
Medicine **Biology** Music **Ancient
Egypt** Evolution Carpentry Physics
Dance Geology **Mathematics** Fitness
Shakespeare **Folklore** Yoga Marketing
Confidence Immortality Biographies
Poetry **Psychology** Witchcraft
Electronics Chemistry History **Law**
Accounting **Philosophy** Anthropology
Alchemy Drama Quantum Mechanics
Atheism Sexual Health **Ancient History**
Entrepreneurship Languages Sport
Paleontology Needlework Islam
Metaphysics Investment Archaeology
Parenting Statistics Criminology
Motivational

The Canterbury Poets.

CONTEMPORARY FRENCH POETRY

Contemporary French Poetry.

Selected and Translated by JETHRO BITHELL.

The Walter Scott Publishing Co., Ltd.

London and Felling-on-Tyne

New York and Melbourne.

1912.

GIFT

To
Henri de Régnier.

"... ceux qui marchent vers la Nuit."—H. de R.

You who interpret Time by symbols rare,
  By hushed lone seas and forests shadow-bound,
  By all the sighings of the soul of sound,
And omens of the soft meandering air—

To unfrequented coasts of Thought you fare,
  And in a land of sadness you have found
  Nature, a nymph who never would be gowned,
And Beauty, who is also proudly bare.

Your pain has sung itself into my breast,
And, hearing you, I know that tears are best,
But tenderness will still them when they throng:

So, o'er a realm whose frontiers never end,
To lure the sad to solace, let me send
Your shadow on a film of ravished song.

—J. B.

CONTENTS.

CONTENTS.

CONTENTS.

INTRODUCTION.

IN 1866 was published at Paris an anthology of verse entitled *Le Parnasse Contemporain.* A second collection appeared under the same title in 1871 ; a third in 1876. The poets thus grouped, between whom and the Romanticists Gautier, Banville, and Baudelaire are the connecting links, came to be known as " Parnassians." In opposition to the personal poetry of the Romantic School, with its apotheosis of the poet's *ego*, and its morbid confessions of feelings most men are fain to hide, the Parnassians preached restraint, the effacement of the artist in his matter, a lofty disdain of cheap sympathy; and they aimed at absolute perfection of form. Most of them, mechanics rather than poets, are now forgotten or discredited ; but the doctrines which they upheld were authoritative in French poetry for twenty years. Two of them, Leconte de Lisle (1818-1894) and José-Maria de Heredia (1842-1905), were great poets; two others, Sully Prudhomme (1839-1910) and François Coppée (1842-1908), achieved an exaggerated reputation. Of the rest, Anatole France and Paul Bourget became successful novelists; while Stéphane Mallarmé, Villiers de l'Isle-Adam, and Paul Verlaine broke a way for a poetry diametrically opposed to the Parnassian manner.

The Parnassian school of poetry was definitely killed about 1885 by a new generation of poets whom their enemies christened "les décadents." Some of them accepted the name; but it fell into disuse among themselves as the term "symbolists" gained ground.

There is a prevalent notion among the ill-informed that the "decadents," or, better, "symbolists" were, or are, perverted voluptuaries, with no more backbone than a lampern, victims of hyperæsthesia, "exquisite invalids," as Anatole France calls them, or, as Ernest Renan said they were, "babies sucking their thumbs." This may be true of such a creature as Maurice Rollinat ("le sous-Baudelaire"), or even of Oscar Wilde, who was in the swim of the movement; but the fact remains that the majority of our symbolists are eminently respectable gentlemen, earnest students who have led as straight a life as many an English Philistine. The reader should disabuse his mind of any prejudice he may have imbibed from such an absurd book as Max Nordau's *Degeneration*,[1] or even Vance Thompson's amusing but misleading *French Portraits*.

The origin of symbolism may be traced back to 1875. In that year the *Parnasse contemporain*

[1] Adolphe Retté relates, in *Le Symbolisme*, how he and his friends got wind of Nordau's plans, sat near him in a café, and regaled him with the most naughty language, telling audacious fibs which he held his deaf ears to drink in, and took for gospel truth. See also the ignorant account in Lombroso's *The Man of Genius*, pp. 230 ff.

refused to include in their third anthology Mallarmé's poem *L'Après-midi d'un Faune*. This appeared separately in 1876, with illustrations by Manet.

ɬ The year before Mallarmé had published a translation of Poe's *Raven*,[1] in a bibliophile's book illustrated also by Manet—a translation into a prose which singularly refines the blatant riming of its original.   In 1876 he published also a reprint of Beckford's *Vathek* (the original French edition of which had been published by a Mallarmé), with a prefatory essay in "symphonic prose."   In 1877 appeared his *Poésies Complètes*, photo-lithographed from the manuscript.   In 1893 his best original work, which had become famous without being known, was made accessible in a volume entitled *Vers et Prose*, with a portrait of the poet by Whistler.

L'Après-Midi d'un Faune inaugurates the revolt against the Parnassian discipline.   Not that the form of the verse presents differences: Mallarmé never rejected the classical prosody.   But the substance was something entirely new ; the poem was the first masterpiece of Symbolism.

What is Symbolism?   The symbolists them-selves have elaborated subtle definitions.   But the

---

[1] Baudelaire's translation of Poe's tales appeared the same year.   Mallarmé published further translations of Poe in 1888.   The over-estimation of Poe in France is astounding. Samain wrote of him (see Bocquet, p. 120): "J'ai lu Poe cette semaine.   Décidément, il est à classer parmi les plus grands . . . Si le mot perfection a pu être prononcé, c'est pour un cas comme celui-là."

b

best definition is perhaps the simplest. *Do not describe; suggest.* "Abolie, la prétention . . . d'inclure au papier subtil du volume autre chose que par exemple l'horreur de la forêt, ou le tonnerre muet épars au feuillage : non le bois intrinsèque et dense des arbres."[1] "Nommer un objet, c'est supprimer les trois quarts de la jouissance du poème, qui est faite du bonheur de deviner peu à peu ; le suggérer, voilà le rêve."[2] For the direct expression of the Parnassians, indirect expression by means of symbols, helped by words revived, or rare, and steeped in mystery, lit with phosphorus from the poet's finger :[3] "d'impollués vocables, la période qui s'arc-boute alternant avec la période aux défaillances ondulées, les pléonasmes significatifs, les mystérieuses ellipses, l'anacoluthe en

---

[1] Mallarmé, *Vers et Prose*, pp. 184-5.

[2] Mallarmé, *Enquête sur l'Évolution littéraire*, p. 60. An extreme example of Mallarmé's method is the line: "Je t'apporte l'enfant d'une nuit d'Idumée"—I bring you the child of an Idumean night, *i.e.*, an Edomite baby, *i.e.*, a poem I have written in the night. Other extreme symbols are those by Saint-Pol-Roux: midwife of light—the cock; sucking sin—a bastard ; to psalm the alexandrine of bronze —to peal midnight; father Adam's cognac—the fresh air; omega—the buttocks : leaves of living salad—frogs.

[3] Rossetti worked at romances of chivalry in the British Museum, hoping to "pitch upon stunning words for poetry" (Knight's *Life of Rossetti*, p. 28). Moréas not only revived words, but actually succeeded in writing the French of Ronsard. Hence the apparent need of the dictionary which a certain Jacques Plowert published in 1888: *Petit Glossaire pour servir à l'Intelligence des Auteurs décadents et symbolistes.*

suspens, tout trope hardi et multiforme . . ."
(Jean Moréas).

Symbolism was also, like the Celtic Revival, a renascence of wonder. In this respect it was a reaction against the naturalistic school which was in vogue in the early eighties.[1] "En ces temps de naturalisme à outrance," says Adolphe Retté,[2] "nous faisions l'effet de troubadours moyenâgeux égarés dans une usine pleine d'odeurs de cambouis et d'huile chaude." The Symbolists were little concerned with things as they are. "Les coraux rouges," says Remy de Gourmont,[3] "nous les vîmes assez: qu'ils soient bleus l" Fancy had been long suppressed, and now there was a subliminal up-rush.

The great fault of the Parnassians is that they paint. "The first concern of the man who writes in prose or verse," says Leconte de Lisle, "should be to set in relief the picturesque side of outer objects." Now Lessing had laid it down in the *Laokoon*, in opposition to the dictum of Horace *ut pictura poësis*, that *genres* in art should not be mixed ; poetry, he said, is in time ; painting and sculpture are in space. But the literature which followed Lessing went against him. Rousseau painted, so did Chateaubriand ; the Romanticists painted, and the Parnassians after them. The Pre-Raphaelites painted, too, though in a different

[1] The bankruptcy of Naturalism dates from the appearance of Viscount Melchior de Vogüé's *Roman russe* in 1885.
[2] *Le Symbolisme*, p. 16.
[3] *L'Idéalisme*, p. 22.

manner to the cold, correct manner of the Par-
nassians; and here let it be said that the Sym-
bolists were influenced by the Pre-Raphaelites,[1]
whose glow of colour several of them have.

But if, according to the rules set up by Lessing,
painting and poetry must not be mixed, neither
must poetry and music. Now the fusing of poetry
and music is the most distinctive mark of symbolist
poetry.[2] Just as Rossetti was at the same time a
painter and a poet, Wagner was at the same time
a composer and a poet. And Wagner, who wrote
fancifully on the mystic marriage of poetry and
music, is one of the fountain-heads of symbolism.[3]

Perhaps they are not wrong who say that music
is the most advanced expression of art: that which
springs from the most refined cultivation of the
mind. If this is true, it follows that as culture
becomes more intense, music will become more
and more its natural medium of expression. But
for the present those who go from the clear poetry
of Tennyson to that of the Symbolists will be
repelled by the obscurity of the latter, vague as
music is.

In the case of Mallarmé the obscurity is de-
liberate. "Mallarmé was an intellectual aristocrat.

---

[1] "D'autres préférences: les poètes anglais Swinburne,
Rosetti (sic), William Morice (sic), le peintre Burne-Jones."
Maeterlinck in Huret's *Enquête*, p. 129.

[2] One might point out, too, the recent confusion of danc-
ing with sculpture and music, and the confusion of music
and sculpture in such a statue as Max Klinger's *Beethoven*.

[3] But see Duhamel and Vildrac, *Notes sur la Technique
poétique*, p. 47.

His tranquil dignity, spiritual poise, politeness without hypocrisy or affectation, his freedom from the usual vulgarities of a society skilled in the art of sensation and puffery, made him conspicuous. But there was method in the obscurity of his literary manner. He was obscure with a purpose. He would make it an impossibility for the critic *à la mode*, be he a Brunetière or a Lemaître, to scale the barriers of his poetic domain."[1]

Sufficient time has already elapsed for us now to be able to estimate the greatness of Mallarmé as against the shallow University critics who ridiculed him. Not that his own work seems likely to be immortal: it is too mannered, extreme, and narrow in range; his real significance lies in the influence he exerted on the generation that followed him. While the professors of the Sorbonne ("ces voix soûles de bruit") were denying the prophet, the brainiest young men of France were drinking in his words. No teacher has ever had such a brilliant or a more devoted band of disciples. They gathered round him in his *salon* in the Rue de Rome : René Ghil, Gustave Kahn, Jules Laforgue, Albert Mockel, Henri de Régnier, Francis Vielé-Griffin, André Fontainas, André Gide, A.-Ferdinand Herold, Pierre Louys, Camille Mauclair, Stuart Merrill, John Payne, Whistler, Adolphe Retté, Marcel Schwob, Paterne Berrichon, and many others who became famous. "Nous passions là des heures inoubliables," says Albert Mockel, "les meilleures,

[1] Francis Grierson.

sans doute, que nous connaîtrons jamais; nous y assistions, parmi toutes les grâces et toutes les séductions de la parole, à ce culte désintéressé des idées qui est la joie religieuse de l'esprit. Et celui qui nous accueillait ainsi était le type absolu du poète, le cœur qui sait aimer, le front qui sait comprendre—inférieur à nulle chose et n'en dédaignant aucune, car il discernait en chacune un secret enseignement ou une image de Beauté."

Probably posterity will consider Mallarmé greater as a man than as a poet; he had more character than genius. Decadent he cannot be called in any sense: he was a gentleman in the best English meaning of the word; his life was stainless, his brain and his senses were healthy. Mockel's book on the master has for its title: *Stéphane Mallarmé. Un Héros.* And a hero he was; not less a hero than Dr. Johnson. But Mallarmé was not like a hedgehog turning its spikes outwards to a hostile world; he was the butt of calumny, malice, and ridicule, but he kept his temper, and did not swerve one hair's breadth from the path he had appointed himself. He had Meredith's scorn of the "critics"; and he did not seek, as so many poets do, to earn his living by poetry, looking upon himself rather as the priest in the temple than as the merchant crying his wares in the market-place. He kept himself and his family by teaching English in various schools: "un labeur de linguistique par lequel quotidiennement sanglote de s'interrompre ma noble faculté poétique."

The confusion of music and poetry was carried

furthest by a poet of Belgian descent, René Ghil (1862-—). He has attempted to write metaphysical poetry on a basis of colour-audition.

His starting-point, no doubt, is Rimbaud's famous sonnet on the vowels; but it must be noted that he does not agree with Rimbaud as to the colours of the vowels I, O, and U, which for him are blue, red, and yellow respectively.

There is nothing at all new in "colour-audition." In 1734 Father Castel invented a *clavecin des couleurs*, a clavichord which was intended "to make sound visible and interpret it in terms of colour."[1] Erasmus Darwin refers to "words of audible music" in the Interlude to Canto II. of his *Loves of the Plants*. Locke mentions a blind person who saw scarlet in the sound of a trumpet (the "scarlet blast of trumpets" is now journalese). Rousseau maintained that "sounds are never more effective than when they produce the impression of colours." Alfred de Musset argued that *fa* was yellow, *sol* red, a soprano voice blonde, a contralto voice brunette. Carlyle, describing a performance at Drury Lane, wrote: "The murmur swelled up from the whole audience into a passionate burst of approval, the voices of the men rising—in your imagination—like a red mountain, with the women's voices floating round it like a blue vapour, you might say." It is not so very far from this to Saint-Pol-Roux' description of the cock's crow as a sonorous poppy.

---

[1] Babbitt, *The New Laokoon*, p. 54 ff., 174 ff.

There is nothing very new, therefore, in René
Ghil's "instrumentist" theories.   He writes:
"Constatant les souverainetés les Harpes sont
blanches; et bleus sont les Violons mollis souvent
d'une phosphorescence pour surmener les par-
oxysmes; en la plénitude des Ovations les cuivres
sont rouges ; les Flûtes, jaunes, qui modulent
l'ingénu s'étonnant de la lueur des lèvres; et,
sourdeur de la Terre et des Chairs, synthèse
simplement des seuls simples, les Orgues toutes
noires plangorent. . . . ."—(*Traité du Verbe*).

The proof of the pudding is in the eating, and
the reader may see if he can digest this extract
from Ghil's *Dire du Mieux:*

"Du mélange éternel des Morts, d'un point de vie
  qui tend tangentiel son désir de renaître
  au long de l'elliptique Plus,—elles n'ont pas
  créé :
        d'avoir laissé maudire la germure
  de leurs ventres, et de l'avoir vouée aux rites
  de l'expiation l'un de l'autre, de l'Homme
  et du Dieu-Homme,—où, n'étendant que les limites
  du désespoir humain et de la vaine somme
  de l'Univers poussant d'une gésine impure —
  tende à mourir en soi la Vie inassouvie :
  la Vie, que de tout son amas de mémoire
  continue à germer l'Amour ! . . ."

One has the impression, in reading Ghil, that he
is a noble, very gifted poet, but lost and strayed.
Still, the explorers in the virgin forests who never
win to the light, they also, deserve well of humanity.
If one can think in colour, one might also be

expected to think in perfumes. This feat was performed by the German Romanticists.[1] Baudelaire's sonnet, "Correspondences," is one of the holy texts of the symbolists.

> " Nature a temple is, whose pillars sing
>   Words of a tangled melody ; and man
>   Passes through woods of symbols old, which scan,
> With eyes he seems to know, his journeying.
>
> Like echoes long, which, as from far they sigh,
>   Blend in a unity dark and profound,
>   Vast as the night and light, so colour, sound,
> And scent to one another's call reply.
>
> Some perfumes are like babies' flesh, and sing
> As sweet as oboes, shine like prairies green.
> —And others, rich, corrupt, and triumphing,
>
> As : incense, amber, musk, and benzoin,
> Even as a shell infinity condenses,
> Proclaim the transports of the soul and senses."

These theories have even been introduced into the theatre. When Roinard's adaptation of the Song of Solomon was staged by the Théâtre d'Art, A dominated in the first act and the decoration was black ; in the second act E prevailed and the decoration was white, etc. Moreover, Roinard wished for clouds of perfume to be shed over the spectators, corresponding to the verbal sensations he hoped to evoke. Unfortunately the resources of the theatre did not permit of the expense the

[1] Babbitt, *The New Laokoon*, pp. 175-6.

experiment would have entailed. "On se contenta
donc de poster dans l'orchestre deux machinistes
qui pétrissaient de modestes vaporisateurs em-
pruntés au cabinet de toilette de Mme. Fort.
Seuls les nez rangés au premier rang des fauteuils
percevaient quelque arôme. Mais le reste de la
salle ne sentait rien. On s'égaya fort à considérer
le sérieux avec lequel les machinistes maniaient
leurs ustensiles. Puis quelques plaisants se mirent
à renifler de toutes leurs forces, de sorte que le
spectacle s'acheva dans un désordre plutôt drô-
latique."[1] The "first experimental perfume concert
in America," which was given at the Carnegie
Lyceum in New York in 1902, and which under-
took to waft the audience on a series of odours to
Japan, seems also to have had a hilarious ending.[2]

One must also point to the influence of German
philosophy on the Symbolists. "On remarquera,"
says Remy de Gourmont, "que les manifestes de
Jean Moréas sont la traduction des idées de
Schopenhauer. Les poètes symbolistes, hypnotisés
par l'irréalité du monde extérieur, se sont mis à le
créer, avec une magnifique fantaisie." Similarly Jean
de Gourmont: "Le Symbolisme ne fut pas d'abord
une révolution, mais une évolution provoquée par
l'infiltration de nouvelles idées philosophiques.
Les théories de Kant, de Schopenhauer, de Hegel
et de Hartmann commençaient à se répandre en
France: les poètes s'en grisèrent."

---

[1] Retté, *Le Symbolisme*, pp. 200-201.
[2] See Babbitt, *The New Laokoon*, p. 182. Saint-Pol-Roux
calls the perfume of flowers "a song for the nostrils"

The ideas of Schopenhauer had already influenced some of the Parnassians, especially Jean Lahor, who is included in this anthology because by his personal note, as well as by his cult of folk-song, he seems a "poet of to-day." His grandmother was a Danish lady, and he married the daughter of a maid of Kent; he was imbued with Germanic and English culture. While a student at Strasburg he came under the spell of German literature; and Rückert's oriental poetry sent him to Indian literature and Buddhism. He was a friend of William Morris and Burne-Jones, and knew Ruskin. He was not a genuine Parnassian; he has the Symbolists' sense of woman. Rocheblave says of his style: "Elle a les mollesses et les tendresses orientales: elle n'en a pas les éclats excessifs. Les mêmes peintures, qui fournirent à un Leconte de Lisle les couleurs d'une mosaïque d'émaux, donnent chez Lahor le moelleux caressant d'un tapis de Perse."[1] His poem "Intérieur Vénitien" may serve as an example of his occasional Pre-Raphaelitism:

"Derrière ses cheveux entre-croisant ses mains
Pour mieux faire saillir la pointe de ses seins,
Sur un drap de brocart s'étend nue et parfaite
Une femme, et rieuse elle penche la tête
Vers son amant, un grave et fier patricien,
Après avoir ainsi posé devant Titien. ·
Sous le ciel clair on voit par la fenêtre ouverte
Luire le Grand Canal, et trembler dans l'eau verte
Le reflet des palais empourprés par le soir.
Le magnifique, assis près d'un lévrier noir,

---

[1] *Œuvres Choisies*, p. xviii.

Écoute, en caressant des yeux la ligne blanche
Et l'ondulation tranquille de la hanche,
Des instruments lointains qui mêlent leurs accords
Au rythme harmonieux et pur de ce beau corps."

Such poetry as this is not unlike that of some of
the Symbolists—A.-F. Herold's for instance.

Villiers de l'Isle-Adam (1840-89) was rather a
prose-writer than a poet. He is mentioned here
because the Symbolists claim him as their master.[1]

Paul Verlaine (1844-96), who was of Belgian
origin, is often classed among the symbolists, but
he was really a somewhat recalcitrant Parnassian—
at all events as far as his prosody is concerned.
He petrified his contemporaries by turning a
sonnet upside down:

" When I was quite a child to me was given
      The Koh-i-noor, I dwelt in fabulous
      Halls of Darius, Heliogabolus.

  Desire created under roofs of driven
      Gold, in scents and sounds of music dying,
      Harems of houris all around me lying.

---

[1] " Je voyais très souvent Villiers de l'Isle-Adam pendant
les sept mois que j'ai passés à Paris. . . .   Tout ce que j'ai
fait, c'est à Villiers que je le dois, à ses conversations plus
qu'à ses œuvres que j'admire beaucoup d'ailleurs."—MAETER-
LINCK, Huret's *Enquête*, p. 128.   " . . . en abandonnant
M. Zola, les jeunes gens savaient qui suivre. Leur maître
(je parle spécialement des plus idéalistes d'entre nous)
était Villiers de l'Isle-Adam, cet évangéliste du rêve et de
l'ironie. . . ."—REMY DE GOURMONT, *ibid.*, p. 135.

My ardent heart, by reason now controlled,
  Knows life, and knows how much it must resign,
  And now it holds in check its folly fine,
Although it is not over much consoled.

Well! If the fates magnificence withhold,
  Fie on all rubies and the dregs of wine,
  On lovely women who can not be mine,
Fie on rich rimes and prudent friends grown cold."

But his substance, of course, was new, and he is
the one God by whom all the symbolists swear.
His "Art poétique" is another of their holy texts:

" Music as rich as the rose is,
    Not equal lines pair by pair,
    But floating vague in the air,
With nothing that weighs down or poses.

Let not thy keen brain be racked
    For words that cannot be wrong:
    Dearest the drunken song
That marries vague to exact.

Veils making lovelier eyes,
    Noon's shivering heat, and in warm
    Autumn evenings the swarm
Of stars shining clear in the skies.

We need but the shade, but the gleam,
    No colour, but chastened lights!
    Only the shade unites
Clarion to flute, dream to dream.

From murderous puns turn thy face,
    And from obscene laughter, and wit,
    The eyes in the blue laugh at it,
All this garlic for appetites base!

O the crimes of rime they are vile !
  What crazy negro, deaf boy,
  Forged us this farthing toy
Ringing hollow under the file ?

Give us music more than of rimes !
  Let thy verse be a thing in the skies,
  Be it felt that a spirit flies
To other loves, other climes.

Let thy verse be the quest of a hint,
  The crisp breeze of morning that blows,
  Sipping the thyme and the rose . . .
All besides is but paper and print."

That poem is worth more than all the commentaries on symbolism. "*La chanson grise*"
(whether it means "gray song," as some of my
friends say, or "drunken song," as others say—but
surely it means both), that is the best description
of many of the best poems which the symbolists
have written, those intangible songs which so often
bring tears to the eyes:

  " Écoutez la chanson bien douce
    Qui ne pleure que pour vous plaire,
    Elle est discrète, elle est légère,
  Un frisson d'eau sur de la mousse ! "

But what blasphemy Verlaine's indictment of
rime must have seemed to the Parnassians ! The
rime was everything to them. Heredia exhausted
history to find such rimes as " bîva—Tokungawa,"
" Bègle—seigle." And this is the way he talked to
Huret: " Une rime heureuse arrivant au bout d'un

beau vers, c'est quelque chose comme le panache
ou la frange d'écume qui parachève, avec un fracas
de tonnerre ou un murmure délicieux, le déferle-
ment d'une belle lame." What would Heredia
have given for the assonances of Francis Jammes?
And yet these assonanced poems of Jammes are
palpitating masterpieces, red with a rich heart's
blood, while Heredia's sonnets are the cold, jewelled
trophies of a life's hard labour.

Arthur Rimbaud, too, is remarkable for his
originality. This wonderful boy ran away re-
peatedly from his home in the Ardennes, lured
like a moth by the glamour of the capital. At
the age of seventeen he had already written his
best poems, and he had the idea of sending these
to Verlaine, who invited him to come to Paris.
He arrived there in 1871, and was Verlaine's guest
for a time. Then the two poets travelled together
in England and Belgium, until Verlaine attempted
to shoot his friend, and was sentenced to two
years' imprisonment. Rimbaud was expelled from
Belgium, went to London to teach English, travelled
in Germany and Italy, enlisted in the Dutch army,
deserted, wandered about the islands of Java, came
back to Europe, became check-taker to a circus,
in which capacity he travelled over England,
Belgium, Holland, and Sweden, and finally, with
funds provided by his family, sailed for Alexandria
with the intention of becoming a merchant. He
arrived in Abyssinia, where he traded with the
natives of the interior, doing good work, too, as an
explorer, and furnishing the Negus with arms to

fight. Italy with.   In 1891 a tumour in his right
knee obliged him to return to France, and he died
in hospital at Marseilles in the same year.

He had written nothing after the poems of his
adolescence, and his book of prose-poetry, *Les
Illuminations* (1886).   The audacity[1] of some of
his poems is appalling—*e.g.*, *Les premières com-
munions:*

> " Vraiment, c'est bête, ces églises de villages
>   Où quinze laids marmots, encrassant les piliers,
>   Ecoutent, grasseyant les divins babillages,
>   Un noir grotesque dont fermentent les souliers " . . .

Not until 1886 did iconoclasts arrive who attacked
the most sacred laws of French poetry.   As every-
body knows, the classical medium of French verse
is the alexandrine.   We all remember with pain
the sing-song tragedies we read at school:

> " Mon épouse, en ces lieux, bien que neuf fois féconde,
>   A pourtant conservé sa grâce pudibonde " . . .

What the men of the new school substituted for
this "whetstone of the teeth" (as Byron called it)
came to be known as the *vers libre*.   Translate the
term, and you explain the thing: it is "free verse."
A bundle of rusty rules are scrapped, and the
length of the line is fitted to the emotion.

[1] "Il y a dans son œuvre plusieurs pages qui donnent un
peu l'impression de beauté que l'on pourrait ressentir devant
un crapaud congrûment pustuleux, une belle syphilis ou
le Château Rouge à onze heures du soir."—REMY DE
GOURMONT.

Who invented the *vers libre?* Some say Rimbaud, in his prose-poems *Les Illuminations.* Others say Jules Laforgue brought it from Germany. Others : Vielé-Griffin set the fashion by some translations from Walt Whitman [1] which he published in *La Cravache.* Some say Marie Krysinska. Gustave Kahn says : Gustave Kahn.

Gustave Kahn, like André Spire, is a Jew. He was born, as Verlaine was, at Metz ; he studied at the *École des langues orientales,* and spent his four years of military service in Algeria. On his return to Paris he founded a weekly journal, *La Vogue,* in which he published most of the poems which appeared in volume form in 1887 as *Les Palais Nomades.* It is a very original and a very obscure book, and it owed more to the poet's Oriental studies and to his Jewish blood than to French tradition. His style grows gradually somewhat clearer in his succeeding books : *Chansons d'Amant* (1891) ; *Domaine de Fée* (1895) ; *La Pluie et le beau Temps* (1895) ; *Limbes de Lumière* (1895) ; and *Le Livre d'Images* (1897).

[1] "A qui doit-on le vers libre ? . . . surtout à Walt Whitman, dont on commençait alors à goûter la licence majestueuse."—REMY DE GOURMONT, *Promenades littéraires,* p. 245. ". . . un des résultats de l'influence de poètes étrangers, notamment du poète américain Walt Whitman, très apprécié des écrivains symbolistes."—*Poètes d'Aujourd'hui,* i., p. 204. "And just as Poe created modern French prose, Whitman re-created modern French verse."—VANCE THOMPSON, *French Portraits,* p. 103. See also Léon Bazalgette's preface to his translations of Whitman, *Feuilles d'Herbe,* Mercure de France, 2nd edit., 1909.

One may read Kahn with wild delight and only understand a word here and there. It is like listening to music:

> " Les voix redisaient: la chanson qui brise
>   en son cœur, son cœur enseveli
>   c'est le son des flûtes aux accords des brises
>   et la marche nuptiale des pâles lys."

Omitted punctuation tangles the sense, there is that hiding of the rimes which was no secret to Wolfram von Eschenbach; but pierce his obscurity, you will find opulent thought and luxuriant, richly-perfumed imagination; and if you have ears to hear, you will find that his music is independent of any rimes he may use, softened by the soothing words he revives, far-wafted from a harp hung on willows, glimpsing strange dream-flowers that rise out of it like lilies. He has the secret of Oriental images—psalms grown silent, rituals of tribes in exile, words at evening on the mountain, Solomon's dazzling song again; a very *débris* of ideas; Jewish sensuality refined on the cold heights of philosophy. His verses are a sea lapping the hard rocks of our incredulity, and now and then one deep-drawn wave curls high and whelms us with emotion.

A translator who produces an anthology like the present must make bold to translate anything, if he is to allot to each poet the space which is due to him among his fellows. But Jules Laforgue defies translation, for the simple reason that his strength lies to a great extent in puns and distortions of meaning. How is one to reproduce *voluptés à vif; la céleste eternullité; Ah! que la vie est quotidienne; chant-huant?* Laforgue's punning is not that which Verlaine condemned, the punning which makes the angels weep—it is a tragic punning, full of the utmost despair, a forlorn gaiety.

It must be made clear, therefore (to those who have not read George Moore's fine appreciation), that of all contemporary French poets there is none more important than Jules Laforgue.[1]

He was born at Montevideo in 1860, of Breton stock. He spent about five years at Berlin as reader to the Empress Augusta, and here, no doubt, familiarized himself with Eduard von Hartmann's *Philosophie des Unbewuszten* (1869), which, with much of Darwin, Schopenhauer, and Buddhism, permeates his ideas. He is the most cerebral, the most logical of French poets.

> " Moi, je suis le Grand Chancelier de l'analyse,
>   Qu'on se le dise . . ."

he says of himself. He is all cynicism, using the language of everyday life, tags and refrains and slang, to eliminate any hint of sentiment from his

[1] "La mort de Laforgue était, pour les lettres, irréparable; il emportait la grâce de notre mouvement, une nuance d'esprit varié, humain et philosophique; une place est demeurée vide parmi nous. C'était le pauvre Yorick qui avait un si joli sourire . . . c'était un musicien du Grand Tout, un passereau tout transpercé d'infini . . ."—GUSTAVE KAHN.

verse. And yet the feeling heart he had can be heard in such a letter as this, written to his sister from Berlin:

"T'ai-je parlé cet hiver d'une jeune Anglaise, avec qui j'avais pris quelques leçons de prononciation? Eh bien, c'est avant-hier au soir que nous, nous sommes fiancés. Depuis avant-hier, ma vie ne m'appartient plus seul, et je sens toute la grandeur de cette idée . . . je ne l'ai pas encore embrassée; hier j'étais assis près d'elle en voiture, dans la soirée, et en la regardant l'idée m'est venue que je pourrais caresser ses cheveux,—j'en ai eu le vertige . . ."

He married his English bride in London on the 31st of December 1886. He died of consumption on the 20th of August 1887, in the twenty-seventh year of his age. His wife had caught the disease from him, and died eight months after his death.

Before his pen had gleaned his teeming brain. And, knowing that he was dying, he could mock at himself in this manner:

" Allons, dernier des poètes,
Toujours enfermé tu te rendras malade!
Vois, il fait beau temps, tout le monde est dehors,
Va donc acheter deux sous d'ellébore,
Ça te fera une petite promenade."

To many French patriots Henri de Régnier is the greatest of living French poets.[1] He himself has publicly given that title to Verhaeren. Verhaeren is richer in ideas, and the more daring in speculation;

---

[1] " Le premier et le plus célèbre des poètes d'aujourd'hui." *Poètes d'Aujourd'hui*, ii., p. 113.

de Régnier is perhaps the more perfect artist. Verhaeren is in the world we live in, de Régnier in a world of dreams. He has not the fresh-air fragrance of Francis Jammes, nor that sadness of the poet of Orthez, which lingers like a perfume in the brain; but he has an inevitability in his subtlest rhythms and a penetrating melancholy of his own which entitle him to be first in the choir of native-born French poets.

His ancestry was noble, and is enumerated in *Poètes d'Aujourd'hui*. His first books were in the Parnassian manner; the real Régnier begins with *Poèmes anciens et romanesques* (1890), mostly in *vers libres*. *Les Jeux rustiques et divins* followed in 1897; *Les Médailles d'Or* in 1900; *La Cité des Eaux* in 1902; *Le Miroir des Heures* in 1911. His three last collections show a constant tendency to return integrally to Parnassian rigours.

His poetry is so uniformly excellent that selection is torture. It has been pointed out that his sense of smell, of hearing, and of sight is very highly developed. Lines in proof may be taken anywhere:

"Avec la double odeur de la chair et du soir
Et les souffles épars comme des chevelures . . ."[1]

"Faunesses dont la lèvre sanglante a l'ardeur
Des grandes roses qui survivent à l'orage . . ."[2]

---

[1] *Poèmes, 1887-1892*; *Mercure de France*, 1895.
[2] *Ibid.*

"Satyresses dont la main folâtre saccage
  Les lys présomptueux qui frôlent leurs genoux,
  Celles de qui le rire est un oiseau sans cage . . ."[1]

His painting of passion has not the full-blooded reek and glow of Verhaeren, who sings his rustic lovers "gaming in a gap of sunshine"; it has a more refined sensuousness, a more imaginative thrill:

"And through dark days till April smiled again
  I loved you with a love so weak and vain
  I needed nothing less to make me bold

In love's most frenzied vehemence to catch
  Your swooning body, than this moss-grown patch,
  Beside yon great ram with the horns of gold."[2]

He is cunning in accumulating the magic of the last line; a disciple, here, of Heredia:

"Ainsi j'ai triomphé de Toi dans l'autre obscur
  Ouvrant sa baie énorme et ronde sur l'azur . . .
  Et nous restions, au bruit des houles murmurantes,

À suivre, en son déclin rayant le ciel plus clair
  Parmi l'effacement des étoiles mourantes,
  La comète aux crins d'or qui tombait dans la Mer."[3]

He is a pessimist:

"Le vrai sage est celui qui fonde sur le sable
  Sachant que tout est vain dans le temps éternel
  Et que même l'amour n'est guère plus durable
  Que le souffle du vent ou la couleur du ciel."

---

[1] *Poèmes, 1887-1892 ; Mercure de France, 1895.*
[2] *Sites*, 1887.   [3] *Ibid.*

But there is comfort in dreams. "A l'appel du poète, les formes naissent et c'est la nudité des nymphes qui se dessine; elles se penchent vers son visage et baisent ses lèvres; elles sont ce qu'il veut, celle qu'il regrette et celle qu'il désire. Tout est d'une égale illusion, et peut-être que les plus vivantes joies sont celles que nous imaginons."[1]

He is haunted by the word "naked" as Mallarmé is haunted by the word "azure." And it is a naked woman (ideal beauty) who, in what is perhaps his most superb poem, "Le Vase,"[2] sets the dreamer his task:

> "Des femmes nues
> Passèrent en portant des paniers et des gerbes,
> Très loin, tout au bout de la plaine.
> Un matin, j'en trouvai trois à la fontaine
> Dont l'une me parla. Elle était nue.
> Elle me dit : Sculpte la pierre
> Selon la forme de mon corps en tes pensées,
> Et fais sourire au bloc ma face claire ;
> Ecoute autour de toi les heures dansées
> Par mes sœurs dont la ronde se renoue,
> Entrelacée,
> Et tourne et chante et se dénoue."

Régnier married, in 1896, Heredia's second daughter, who is the distinguished novelist "Gérard d'Houville." Her poems have not yet appeared in volume form.

Jean Moréas is perhaps destined to live in

---

[1] Jean de Gourmont, *Henri de Régnier*, p. 32.
[2] *Les Jeux rustiques et divins.*

literary history as the classical example of auto-
latry. Vance Thompson reports his conversation
as follows:—"It was I who invented symbolism
. . . and now I abolish it; the decree has gone
forth—there is no symbolism more . . . I have
found another name for my school, and now my
poetry is the *poésie romane.* It covers the art of
the *midi* of Europe—that art which has reached
its highest development in French literature . . .
I have always been a rebel. The fierce blood of
the klepht is in my veins. I am a Greek—in fact
I believe I am the last representative of the true
Greek race. My family is of Epirus. It is illus-
trious. It is called Papadiamantopoulos . . . I
am Son-of-a-Diamond-in-whose-family-was-a-priest
. . . My race engenders heroes . . . My father
wished to send me to Germany to school. I
revolted. I wished to see France. Twice I ran
away from home—at last I reached Paris. Destiny
pointed the way—my star led me—to become the
greatest of French poets."

Now, Moréas, with his moustache of the blue
gleams which poets sang, is already a saga, but
it is easy, by turning to what he wrote, to see
how untrue such alleged rodomontades must be.
As a matter of fact, his poetry is fascinating,
and his prose is not less so. Jean Moréas may
not have been the genius he thought he was,
but he was, at all events, one of the most brilliant
men of his time. It was no imbecile whom the
Muses laughed at who could write such a poem
as " Remembrances":

" D'où vient cette aubade câline
Chantée—on eût dit—en bateau,
Où se mêle un pizzicato
De guitare et de mandoline ?

Pourquoi cette chaleur de plomb
Où passent des senteurs d'orange,
Et pourquoi la séquelle étrange
De ces pèlerins à froc blond ?

Et cette Dame, quelle est elle,
Cette Dame que l'on dirait
Peinte par le vieux Tintoret
Dans sa robe de brocatelle ?

Je me souviens, je me souviens :
Ce sont des défuntes années,
Ce sont des guirlandes fanées,
Et ce sont des rêves anciens l " [1]

As to his *poésie romane*, his thesis was : Nothing
is admirable outside of the Greek and Latin tradi-
tion. But Shakespeare is admirable : therefore
Shakespeare was an Italian. . . .[2]

Like de Régnier, he returned in his last work
to the classical style, and wrote the laboriously
ordinary poetry of his *Les Stances* (1901).

Ernest Raynaud, with several others, rallied
round the banner of the *Ecole romane*. In his
volume of verse *La Couronne des Jours* there are
charming sonnets on cities. The following, of
Brighton, is spoiled by a grotesque rime (but

[1] *Les Syrtes*, 1884.
[2] See Retté, *Le Symbolisme*, p. 117.

Verlaine rimed "brouillard" with "Salford," and
Louis Thomas, who also is an English scholar,
rimes "Albemarle" with "voiles" and "Beardsley"
with "brisées"); it is not one of his best, but it will
interest Englishmen:

> " Le soir meurt lentement sur l'écume apaisée ;
> Une rousse buée enveloppe la mer ;
> Un reflet de Venise a doré le ciel vert ;
> Un bruit d'instruments sonne aux barques pavoisées.
>
> Autour de la jetée aux brûlantes croisées,
> Les sports font leur rumeur énergique dans l'air.
> (Triomphant d'une image abondante exposée,
> Sandow ici s'égale en gloire à lord Robert.)
>
> Mâle Albion, ruée aux vagues élastiques,
> J'ai vu luire dans l'ombre, aux lueurs des musiques,
> De ton beau rêve nu le sombre diamant !
>
> Et j'imagine—avec l'assentiment de l'heure—
> Un dieu broyant un tigre entre ses bras fumants,
> Tandis qu'un long goût d'âle et de whisky demeure."

The prevailing note in the French poetry of the
nineteenth century is that of sadness. Paul Fort
is glad and gay; but he is the god Pan, and even
his reed sounds split sometimes. Alfred de Vigny
and Baudelaire were full of despair and passionate
blasphemy. Leconte de Lisle was a Nihilist.
Mallarmé had renounced the world, the flesh, the
devil, and the professors of poetry. Verlaine and
Rimbaud were waifs and strays. Francis Jammes
is sick with nostalgic regret. Samain and Charles

Guérin died of sadness. For de Régnier life is the dream of a shadow . . .

Is all this black pessimism the despair of a decaying race? One is tempted to entertain the thought when one looks from France to Germany and sees the exuberant optimism of the poets who have heard the voice of Zarathustra. And again, when one finds that the only voices of confidence in the future were for a long time those of two Flemings, Verhaeren and Maeterlinck; voices which have now awakened others among the younger generation of French poets, those of the Abbey group. But we must give up the idea of a decaying race, and believe that the pessimism of the nineteenth century is a thing of the past, when we find that mordant young cynic Pierre Lièvre writing, in a book just published: "Parmi nos contemporains, il n'y a pas un seul désespéré. Chacun trouve la vie belle. Quelle sotte résignation."

The French symbolists are sad. But two of them are Americans, Francis Vielé-Griffin (the son of General Vielé-Griffin, of New York), and Stuart Merrill. And Vielé-Griffin has been called "the poet of joy." Of a grey joy, it is true; he sings of gladness with a veiled voice.

His first book, *Cueille d'Avril,* appeared in 1886. He published a prose translation of Swinburne's *Laus Veneris* in 1895, and he was the first to introduce Walt Whitman to the French public. More than his translations, his original verse has been a powerful agent in the introduction of English rhythms into French poetry. He is indeed (as Albert Mockel is also) a very prince of rhythm; "his verse unwinds with the suppleness of waving scarfs." He has learned much from folk-songs, the refrains of which he imitates with masterly effect.

When one reads Verhaeren one catches oneself saying: How sonorous that would have been in Flemish! One feels how the Flemish language would have suited Maeterlinck's mysticism. But when one reads Vielé-Griffin and Stuart Merrill, although one hears subconscious and familiar cadences, one is certain that only French could give these delicate shades; both poets have, by the mere chance of their French education (and the same may be said of Jean Moréas), the medium which exactly fits their genius. The saddening thought for us is this: that English literature has lost to France two delicate and fascinating poets, who might have stood by the side of W. B. Yeats and Arthur Symons as wizards of the word. And the United States have lost their two greatest contemporary poets.

Stuart Merrill was born on Long Island, Walt Whitman's country. He was educated at the Lycée Condorcet in Paris, and among his schoolfellows there were André Fontainas, René Ghil, and Pierre Quillard. He returned to New York to study law, but wrote his first book, *Les Gammes*, instead. This fascicle of sixty pages was printed by Vanier at Paris in 1887; full of that Swinburnian alliteration ("Car le vœu du viol m'envenime les veines ") which he and Vielé-Griffin have made part and parcel of contemporary French poetry, it struck a new note, and gave a promise of better things which his development amply fulfilled.

Like Verhaeren, Vielé-Griffin, and André Spire, he is a Socialist poet; indeed, while his verse was appearing in France, he was organizing the Socialist groups in America.

But his poetry is by no means democratic. It appeals only to such Socialists as Arnold Bennett. It is above all learned, exquisitely refined, scintillant with the jewels of rare words. Take "Celle qui prie":

> " Ses doigts gemmés de rubacelle
> Et lourds du geste des effrois
> Ont sacré d'un signe de croix
> Le samit de sa tunicelle,
>
> Sous ses torsades où ruisselle
> La rançon d'amour de maints rois,
> Sa prunelle vers les orfrois
> Darde une viride étincelle.
>
> Et c'est par l'oratoire d'or
> Les alléluias en essor
> De l'orgne et du violoncelle
>
> Et, sur un missel à fermail
> Qu'empourpre le soir d'un vitrail,
> Ses doigts gemmés de rubacelle." [1]

In *Les Fastes* (1891), as in *Les Gammes*, there is more outward ornamentation of poems, jewelled

----

[1] Poèmes, 1887-97.

and empty vessels to dazzle the eyes, than draughts
from those vessels to reach the heart; but in *Les
Quatre Saisons* (1900) it is the heart's tenderness
which makes them good to know.   Time and trial
have made him riper, sweeter, and far more sad;
and in his last collection, *Une Voix dans la Foule*
(1909), it is the regret of things outlived that
moves us most; now he thrills us from a violin,
whereas once he filled us with organ notes.   This
poem, which he calls "Mourir," might have been
written by that laureate of even-chimes, Grégoire
le Roy:

> " Ici, devant la fenêtre
> De la chambre bleue et grise
> D'où je vois l'orme et le hêtre
> Se balancer sous la brise,
>
> J'arrête un peu ma faiblesse
> Qu'enfièvre le crépuscule,
> Doux malade que tout blesse
> Et qui devant tout recule.
>
> C'est l'heure molle des rêves,
> Des larmes et des silences,
> Des souvenances trop brèves
> Et des lentes somnolences.
>
> Les fleurs, sous la moindre haleine,
> S'éparpillent sur le sable.
> Mais je me désole à peine
> De savoir tout périssable.
>
> La Mort même sait sourire.
> Ce rideau blanc devient rose.
> Je ne sais si je respire
> Ni si je sens quelque chose.

Mourir serait si facile
Au bruit léger de la brise,
Mourir quand le jour vacille
Dans la chambre bleue et grise ! " [1]

Merrill is the poets' poet and the poets' friend. It is easy even for a stranger to guess at the love with which his fellow-singers surround him.

All the poets love Stuart Merrill. Everybody loves Francis Jammes. You will worship some of the poets, at a distance. If one were to see Francis Jammes, one would be sure to go to him with outstretched hand, saying: Comment allez-vous, monsieur Jammes?

He *will* keep telling you that he is Francis Jammes. He could not have found anything more interesting to write about. There is only one Francis Jammes. And he lives at Orthez, at the foot of the Pyrenees. There are "men of talent" in Paris . . .

Do not open his books, if you believe in the *gradus ad Parnassum.* He knows nothing about it. You will say his rimes are worse than Mrs. Browning's, if you swear by rimes, like the troubadours long, long ago; but if an assonance can reach your heart, you will perhaps come to think that there is only one poet, and he is Francis Jammes. [2]

He was a notary's clerk once. He wrote some verses, which he dedicated to Hubert Crackanthorpe.

---

[1] *Une Voix dans la Foule,* p. 47.

[2] "Dès qu'on se laisse aller (à Jammes), il semble que lui seul soit poète." André Gide, *Prétextes.*

They were discovered by "men of talent" at Paris.
He was famous after that.   The "men of talent"
have now defined "le Jammisme."   You understand
he is the founder of a "school" of poetry.   He has
his disciples; the best are Thomas Braun and
Victor Kinon, those good catholics of Flanders.
But what is "le Jammisme".?   Let him tell you
himself: "Mon Dieu, vous m'avez appelé parmi les
hommes.   Me voici, je souffre et j'aime.   J'ai parlé
avec la voix que vous m'avez donnée.   J'ai écrit
avec les mots que vous avez enseignés à ma mère et
à mon père qui me les ont transmis.   Je passe sur
la route comme un âne chargé dont rient les enfants
et qui baisse la tête."

And here is a definition by a man of talent in
Paris.   "Tout l'effort que d'autres font pour parer
leur pensée de riches ornements, il le met, au
contraire, à la dévêtir de tout enjolivement.   Il la
veut présenter toute nue.   Et, pour être plus sûr
de ne la point dissimuler sous la vaine beauté des
rythmes et des images, il préfère n'employer que
des mètres inégaux, brisés, dénués de cette in-
volontaire harmonie que donne la juste application
des règles habituelles."[1]

You will see that he compares himself to an
ass.   Perhaps you will laugh at that.   The more
fool you.   You will not laugh if your heart goes out
to the asses, as the heart of Francis Jammes does.
Those good gray asses, gray as the dust .of the
plains under the Pyrenees . . .

He loves all animals, and insects.   And flowers,

[1] Beaunier, p. 336.

and all that grows in the open air. He is *the* bucolic poet.

There is one of God's creatures that he loves best of all. " . . . voici que, dans ce décor agreste, multiple et divers, parmi la faune, la flore et les forêts, le long des eaux, un être plus charmant que l'écureuil et les bécassines, plus souple que le lièvre, mieux paré que le martin-pêcheur des rives, aussi frais que la renouée-liseron des bois, apparaît dans la fine beauté des violettes. Cet être, fait de lumière et de lait, sentant le foin et le miel, d'une ingénue grâce, nue comme Chloé surprise ou vêtue de vieilles étoffes à ramages, coiffée d'un chapeau fleuri, c'est la jeune fille des poésies de Francis Jammes."[1]

His books are flowered with girls as hedgerows are with wild roses :

" Car j'aime comparer à de très jeunes filles
      mes pensées qui ont la courbe de leurs jambes craintives . .

They have never bored him :

" Les jeunes filles ne m'ennuyèrent jamais :
      vous savez qu'elles vont, d'où se sait quoi, causer
      le long des tremblements de pluie des églantiers

(That last line is as much a miracle as Tennyson s : " The pillared shade of sounding sycamores "). And since he is burning with health, and since they laugh at Mrs. Grundy in France, he does not put a leaf before his mouth.

[1] Edmond Pilon, *Francis Jammes*, pp. 33-34.

d

He is not always humble (like the good, grey asses); there is a void in him that reveries cannot fill, and it makes him so very, very sad. (You go haunted by his sadness when you have read him. Nothing can console you.) All God's things suffer . . . and he is moved by "un épi malade parmi les épis sains." He has a passion for the past, for the days of Rousseau and Bernardin de Saint Pierre:

"C'est aujourd'hui la fête de Virginie . . .
Tu étais nue sous ta robe de mousseline.
Tu mangeais de gros fruits au goût de Mozambique
et la mer salée couvrait les crabes creux et gris.

Ta chair était pareille à celle des cocos.
Les marchands te portaient des pagnes couleur d'air
et des mouchoirs de tête à carreaux jaune-clair.
Labourdonnais signait des papiers d'amiraux.

Tu es morte et tu vis, ô ma petite amie,
amie de Bernardin, ce vieux sculpteur de cannes,
et tu mourus en robe blanche, une médaille
à ton cou pur, dans la *Passe de l'Agonie*."

And then he is home-sick for the tropics. His grandfather was a physician at Guadeloupe, you know, and was ruined by the earthquake there, and came back:

"n'ayant qu'un souvenir de femme dans le cœur . . ."

He keeps this grandfather's old letters in a drawer. He is always dreaming of the Jammes who are dead ; and the old furniture which was theirs, and is now his, speaks to him . . .

He is a man, as Walt Whitman was. More complicated, as one must expect a Frenchman to be. But teaching us, as Whitman does, to be natural, and to live freely in the open air. How much nobler than *ære perennius* is this :

"Je ne suis qu'un homme. Et c'est là ma grandeur.
Je vais bientôt vieillir comme d'autres vieillirent
ayant, de jour en jour, de moins en moins compris
ce qui me distingua d'un simple laboureur."

Jammes is a poet of the tropics from afar (how could he leave Orthez? Amsterdam or Algeria, just a glance . . . but then back to Orthez). A poet who has seen the tropics is John-Antoine Nau. He was born at San Francisco (when, he has not told us).

The prosody of Jammes (or rather his lack of it) is all his own. Equally original, at first sight, seems the metrical form adopted by Paul Fort. Like Jammes, he is a sensuous poet and reflects the outer world. But whereas Jammes is subjective, Fort is objective.

Paul Fort was a boy of eighteen, an "éphèbe audacieux," when, in 1890, he founded the Théâtre d'Art, which staged unknown masterpieces (Shelley's *Cenci*, Marlowe's *Faust*, Maeterlinck's *L'Intruse* and *Les Aveugles*, van Lerberghe's *Les Flaireurs*, etc.), and which developed into the " Œuvre." Three years later he began to publish his astonishing "ballades," "prose-poems," or "rhythmic prose," sometimes rimed and sometimes not.

The " prose-poem," at its worst, is easy to write.

Like the hexameter which the railway companies publish: "Passengers are requested to keep their feet off the cushions," it may be written unawares. In witness whereof the following (not an advertisement here) from the *Daily Mail :*

"'The calendar assures us this is May. A month, so far, of ills and chills and grievous treachery ; a month whose lesson plainly reads ' Beware.'
Let Wolsey help you—Wolsey underwear . . .
We all know how a chill begins ; who can predict its end ?
Wear wool next to your skin—humanity itself can find naught else so good, and Wolsey Underwear is Wool.
So wear it; wear it as you value health . . . wear Wolsey night and day."

This metrical composition has all the elements of a good "prose-poem." It has assonances : May — beware ; good — wool ; one *rime riche :* (Be)ware—(Under)wear ; and a sufficient rime : (be)gins—skin.

It is quite evident that Paul Fort turns out his "ballades" as easily as an organ-grinder turns out his tunes. The terrible amount he has written proves his facility. But any other person would find it very difficult to write such poems ; he would need Paul Fort's undoubted genius to begin with.

The verse never stumbles. Critics have suggested that it is so smooth because it is regular, and that, in short, Paul Fort is a wolf in sheep's clothing, or a Parnassian masquerading as a *vers-libriste.* There is, in fact, nothing very irregular except the continuous typographical arrangement ;

divide the lines in the usual manner of verse (as a translator may be permitted to do with his translations), and there will be nothing to make a conservative's hair stand on end.

"C'est un homme très extraordinaire que Paul Fort," says André Beaunier in the best book of essays yet written about the symbolists. "Il ne fait partie d'aucune école; il ne se piête à nulle classification. Il frappe d'abord par sa désinvolture, sa spontanéité, le sans-gêne singulier de sa manière, une sorte d'excessive abondance. Quand on se demande à qui l'apparenter, on lui trouve de la ressemblance surtout avec le dieu Pan . . ."

Fort is the editor of *Vers et Prose*, which he founded in 1905. This review and the *Mercure de France* are indispensable to students of contemporary literature.

The Countess de Noailles is a singer of gardens and orchards; but a very different one to Jammes. He is a wild flower scenting the sunlight; she is a dazzling orchid in Parisian *salons*.

It is difficult to decide of what nationality she is. Her grandfather was a Wallachian hospodar who married a Moldavian princess of Greek stock. Her mother, the Princess de Brancovan, was the daughter of Musurus Pasha, *olim* Turkish ambassador in London; her sister became Princess de Chimay.

Madame de Noailles has published novels as well as poetry. Her enemies have christened her "Madame Réclamier."

Some of her best poems are those in which she

dreams of "tattered rhymesters." This is legend
reversed; instead of Villon riming the ladies of
old time, of Alain Chartier with the kiss of Margaret
of Scotland on his dreaming face, we have now the
"Princesse lointaine" singing to the dear outcasts:

THE SHADES.

When, having toiled much, I
must bid the world good-bye,
    with sad heart weeping,
I shall go to the lands where dwell
all those who sang songs well,
    their book still keeping.

Dear François Villon, who
sang as the crickets do
    so glad and gay,
how I had loved thee dearly,
thee whom they hanged up nearly
    upon the King's highway.

Verlaine, thou staggering man,
who singest like god Pan
    a satyr's strain,
art thou ever simple and divine,
drunken with fervour and with wine,
    good Saint Verlaine?

And thou whose cruel fate
tracked thee with ruthless hate,
    poor Heinrich Heine,
yet noble life hadst thou,
rest now thy tired brow
    in my hands so tiny.

And I, who still have shared,
more than most women dared,
    all that did sear you . . .
I am so worn and sad,
O my wise gods and mad,
    let me rest near you . . .[1]

We have seen that de Régnier and Moréas, perhaps with an eye to the *Académie Française*, returned to the classical prosody. But the two contemporary French poets who found it possible to write in alexandrines and yet be great writers are Albert Samain and Charles Guérin.

Samain was born at Lille, of poor parents. His father died when he was at school. He was a clerk from his fourteenth year till his death; his ambition was satisfied when he obtained a position at the Town Hall of Paris. He was that rare thing, a modest Frenchman (but in mitigation it must be conceded that he was, like Verlaine, of Flemish descent). He was so modest that he was actually unable to push himself ("se pousser") when opportunity offered. He might easily have won himself a recognized position as one of the first of living Frenchmen: his poetry was hailed with enthusiasm even in his lifetime; but he was a prey to that shyness which is more tormenting than any disease. He wanted to marry, but he had to keep his mother, to whom he was so devoted that her death accelerated his. One cannot read his story without one's heart bleeding.

He taught himself Greek and English. The

---

[1] *L'Ombre des Jours*, Calman-Lévy.

most evident influence in his earlier work is that
of Baudelaire; in his later work, that of Chénier.
He associated with the Symbolists, and with several
of them he founded the *Mercure de France*; but he
never belonged to any school.

During his lifetime he published two volumes of
verse: *Au Jardin de l'Infante* in 1893, and *Aux
Flancs du Vase* in 1898. After his death the
Mercure de France published, in 1901, another
collection of poems, *Le Chariot d'Or*, and a volume
of stories, *Contes*, in 1902.

The majority of our translations are from the
first volume. The second volume contains his
poignant tragedy, *Polyphème*, the lyric throes of
his own despair. The rest of the book contains
so many beautiful poems that one does not know
which to choose; indeed a translator with Samain's
books before him can hardly help translating the
poems one by one as they occur. "Myrtil et
Palémone" has Samain's characteristic note of
ache:

"Myrtil et Palémone, enfants chers aux bergers,
Se poursuivent dans l'herbe épaisse des vergers,
Et font fuir devant eux, en de bruyantes joies,
La file solonnelle et stupide des oies.
Or Myrtil a vaincu Palémone en ses jeux ;
Comme il l'étreint, rieuse, entre ses bras fougueux,
Il frémit de sentir, sous les toiles légères, .
Palpiter tout à coup des formes étrangères ;
Et la double rondeur naissante des seins nus
Jaillit comme un beau fruit sous ses doigts ingénus.
Le jeu cesse . . . Un mystère en son cœur vient d'éclore,
Et, grave, il les caresse et les caresse encore."

Of such a lover as Charles Guérin one feels that he *must* die young. It is Keats over again. "L'art suprême se suicide," said Albert Samain. Such sensitiveness is like consumption. He was thirty-four when he died. He had been tormented by what he called "l'inquiétude de Dieu," and, like Retté and Jammes, he had returned to Roman Catholicism.

Remy de Gourmont is not so much a poet as a prose-writer, and it is no exaggeration to say there is none better in France. Grammarian, philologist, critic, philosopher, novelist, dramatist, his learning is encyclopædic: he is the Diderot of our days. Like Elysée Reclus and Paterne Berrichon, he used to be classed as an Anarchist.

Adolphe Retté, too, was an Anarchist—in his prime. He was one of the most combative of the Symbolists then. Now, he is sure of Heaven.

André-Ferdinand Herold, besides being an excellent poet (a Pre-Raphaelite Symbolist), is a learned Orientalist and a translator from the German.

Pierre Quillard is a Greek scholar, an Orientalist, and a critic. He has remained more or less faithful to the Parnassian prosody. He is shrouded in gloom:

> " Les mains lasses d'avoir cueilli des asphodèles
> Et de sombres pavots qui conseillent la mort."

Paul-Napoléon Roinard is a romance. When he was twenty he ran away from his home at Neufchâtel-en-Bray, arrived in Paris, and wrote thousands of verses which he afterwards destroyed. He published a volume of biographies of future great men, one of whom was himself. Conscious of being an Anarchist, he exiled himself to Brussels; an unnecessary expense, as he seems to have been considered harmless. In Brussels, however, he worked a little, the result being that whereas he had left Paris with five francs in his pocket, he returned with five francs ten centimes. When his book, *La Mort du Rêve*, came out in 1902, a banquet was offered to him, and Rodin presided. His poetry is often wicked, but always inspired by high moral purpose.

Fernand Gregh has been praised by Professor Faguet, but he is genuinely interesting. He has been *Chevalier de la Légion d'honneur* since 1906.

Robert de Souza is rather a theorist and a technician than a poet. In his book *La Poésie populaire et le Lyrisme sentimental* he shows that the poetry of the Symbolists is "popular" like the folk-song, in so far as it is what Wordsworth defined as "the spontaneous overflow of powerful emotions," whereas the planed and varnished verse of Gabriel Vicaire (and Company) is artificial.

Viscount Robert d'Humières is known in England by his book *L'Ile et l'Empire de Grande-Bretagne* (Mercure de France, 1904). He has translated Rudyard Kipling. He is said to have been influenced by Shelley; but he seems to owe more to Ernst Haeckel.

Henri Barbusse, who is the editor of *Je sais tout*, has only published one volume of verse, *Les*

Pleureuses (Fasquelle, 1895), a book full of the rhythms of fading things.

Henry Bataille is well known to London audiences as a dramatist. He is not less distinguished as a lyric poet. His verse is weighted with indolent sadness, a sadness so peculiarly his own that it stamps every line he has written as with a trade-mark. He is the poet of weariness. In Bataille's poems those three full-stops, now such a common device, are worth pages and pages of description. It seems as if his voice failed him, as if these things were too sad to be said, as if words could not paint the heart's dejection. His strains have a dying fall:

VILLAGES.

There are long evenings when the hamlets die,
  After the pigeons have come home to perch.
They die with the day's din, and the blue cry
  Of swallows steepled on the ivied church . . .
Then little lights to watch their death are lit,
  Tapers of nuns in their high-built abode,
And by the misty houses lanterns flit . . .
  Afar winds leisurely the grey high-road . ..
To listen to their village growing cold,
  The flo e s, that love the place where they were
      born, r
Over their mournful hearts their petals fold . . .
  Then are the lights extinguished, while the worn
Familiar walls perish without a sigh,
Easily, as old, simple women die.

Paterne Berrichon, who has married Rimbaud's sister, and written the life and published the letters of that vagrom man, denies that he was ever an anarchist, and calls himself a decadent. His poems are hospital scenes, spasms of refined madness, cries of outlawry. "On déambule sur le *bitume aux verts reflets*, ou bien dans des Edens des femmes s'étreignant

. . . ' Loin des amants maudits dont le torse velu
Piquait leur derme en fleurs de rubis ébriaques.'. . . " . . .

Alfred Mortier was a Symbolist in his drama *La Fille d'Artaban* (1896), but he has latterly deserted to classicism in his tragedy *Marius vaincu* (1910). His volume of verse *Le Temple sans Idoles* (1909) is characterized, mostly, by a rough-hewn style well suited to its ratiocinative Satanism. His jolted verse seems best:

" Je voudrais qu'une femme, au cœur
Subtil et connaissant l'amour,
En feuilletant mes vers un jour,
Dît : ' Ah ! le maladroit rimeur !'

Mais qu'en dépit d'un tel langage,
Prise à certain charme secret,
Elle ne quittât mon livret
Qu'en tournant la dernière page."

Pierre Lièvre's *Jeux de Mots* appeared in 1909, a year which would be memorable if only for the fact that it saw the publication of this volume, of Mortier's *Le Temple sans Idoles*, and of Louis Thomas' *Les douze Livres pour Lily*. The title *Jeux de Mots* is, like the poems which compose it, audacious: for Lièvre "un jeu de mots" is not a pun, but an artful collocation of words—*i.e.*, a poem. The foreign reader is more likely to be fascinated by the substance of these poems, their revelation of a new sensibility, the fibrous thinking of the most modern version of a cynic, than by their mastery of form; but in Lièvre the poet is fortified by the critic. A book of criticism he has just published, *Notes et Réflexions sur l'Art poétique*, should be studied in conjunction with *Notes sur la Technique poétique*, by Georges Duhamel and Charles Vildrac; these two books, written at opposite poles, show the present state of French prosody. Duhamel and Vildrac champion the *vers libre;* Lièvre sees no difference between *vers libres* and prose, but he admits assonance, and rejects several of the Parnassian rules. He is preparing a new series of *Jeux de Mots*, and we have the privilege of first printing the three following poems from it. The first is a sample of the dramatic lyrics he writes, as does also Alfred Mortier:

FIN DE SOUPER.

" Chérie, écoutez-moi, je suis triste, il est tard,
les restes du souper sont épars sur la nappe,
la musique se tait, les lustres sont blafards,
l'inquiétude me gagne : une anxiété me frappe.

Secourez-moi, Chérie, il le faut, inventez
ce que depuis toujours mon désespoir réclame,
je sens, je sens ce soir avec trop d'acuité
que j'ai tout dépassé . . . ah ! j'ai la mort dans l'âme."

Mais la charmante enfant, qui songe à Dieu sait quoi,
sous son chapeau coûteux de grue un peu actrice,
les coudes sur la table et salissant ses doigts
suce indifféremment des pattes d'écrevisse.

EPIGRAMME DANS LE GOÛT DE L'ANTHOLOGIE.

Que ferai-je pour toi, Amour, si tu m'exauces ?
Devrai-je te bâtir en un lieu bien choisi,
un de ces temples clairs dont le fronton se hausse,
    au dessus d'arbres arrondis ?

Pourrai-je t'honorer, avec moins de dépense,
en t'élevant chez moi un autel familier,
ou, accueilleras-tu, pour toute récompense
    deux colombes, et trois rosiers ?

Il n'y a chose au monde, Amour, je te le jure
que je refuse, à ta demande, de vouer,
si ce n'est la moitié de cette chevelure
    que je rêve de dénouer.

PAYSAGE ELYSÉEN.

Sur des arbres que dore un éternel automne
un crépuscule ardent s'allonge infiniment.
Dans un vent tiède et fort des feuilles tourbillonnent
et des rayons pesants tombent du firmament
    limpide et monotone.

La vigne vierge pend du haut des colonnades
dont quelques fûts brisés gisent près des bassins.
Des rosiers tout en fleurs grimpent aux balustrades
et des arbres taillés, par dessus les chemins
    se joignent en arcades.

D'innombrables pigeons animent les corniches
d'un ruineux palais qu'embrase le couchant.
Des statues mutilées y dansent dans des niches.
Quelques paons font traîner sur les perrons penchants
    leur plumages trop riches.

En des lieux si sereins, sous de si beaux ombrages
des êtres radieux, aux calmes attitudes,
se continuent sans fin, immuables et sages,—
—Mais l'ennui souverain de la béatitude
 règne sur leurs visages.

It would be wrong to call Lièvre a "Neo-Parnassian," because, as we have seen, he does not subscribe *in toto* to the metrical doctrines of the Parnassians. But there is a whole crowd of determined rhymesters who may fitly be called "Neo-Parnassians," not because they are slaves to the classical prosody, for some of them are no more bound by it than Lièvre is,[1] but because they have nothing new to say, and no personality to reveal. Scholars and gentlemen, no doubt; but poets, no. Type of these indefatigable aspirants was Auguste Angellier (1848-1911), whose imaginative book on Burns has given some measure of publicity in this country to his dignified, discreet, and ordinary metrical compositions, of which the Clarendon Press has published some selections, including the following:

" Les géraniums, les phlox, les colchiques,
 Les lourds dahlias, et les véroniques,
  Et les verges d'or,

---

[1] ". . . actuellement la plupart des poètes qui 'donnent dans le classique' ne s'accommodent pas des anciennes règles, devenues servitudes, sans une multitude de compromis blessants pour la logique et dont l'hypocrisie puérile fait sourire."—DUHAMEL ET VILDRAC, *Notes sur a Technique poétique.*

Gisent dans l'humus sous les feuilles mortes,
En proie au hideux peuple des cloportes,
    Ouvriers de mort."

Angellier's poetry deserves no more admiration in this country than is vouchsafed to it in France, but there are several poets for whom we have not been able to find space in this anthology who are well worth the scholarly attention of the Clarendon Press; though, it is true, some of them write more frankly wicked verse than Angellier's old book-worm's dreams of adultery.

The task of an anthologist is hard. He has to wade through an interminable wilderness of weeds and flowers, and he must be guided by his sense of smell if he would find flowers to transplant. We have left the sunflowers standing. At the very end of our wanderings we discovered a frail lily flowering in the cold. It was too late to transplant it; but we can tell where it can be found. This white lily among the daffodils, or, to abandon symbolism, the yellow-backs, is a stately volume published in 1909, and part of the series "Les Bibliophiles fantaisistes." It is a book called *Les douze Livres pour Lily*, and its author is Louis Thomas, the æsthete who has translated Arthur Symons.[1] Since Thomas, as he says himself, is perverted (p. 237), there is nothing whatever in his *griffonnages* save love:

---

[1] Arthur Symons, *Poésies*. Bruges: Arthur Herbert Ltd., 1907.

" Un jour, lisant ces vers, je me dirai peut-être :
Quel enfant vous étiez de chanter ces plaisirs,
    O si jeune poète.

Et lors je serai fou, car il ne sert de naître
Si ce n'est pour aimer, pour vivre, pour souffrir,
    Tout ainsi qu'une bête."

He makes art out of his everyday life, effortless
art, gossamer verse, which seems to be saying
πάντα ῥεῖ:

" Je voudrais parler de ces lignes
    Que fait ton corps souple en tournant,
    Mais elles sont si fluides
    Qu'elles ne durent qu'un moment.

Et comme le bruit que fait la feuille
    Lorsqu'elle chante dans le vent,
    C'est un plaisir que l'on accueille
    Et qui s'efface au même instant."

Another excellent poet discovered too late for
insertion among the poets translated is Tristan
Klingsor (1874-—).   He is a painter by profes-
sion ; but he is a musician as well, and has
published music of his own (*Chansons de ma
Mère l'Oie*).   A short play of his, *La Duègne
apprivoisée*, has been acted.   His first collections
of verse (*Filles-fleurs* and *Squelettes fleuris*) are out
of print ; *Schéhérazade* and *Le Valet de Cœur* are
published at f3.50 each by the Mercure de France.
Schéhérazade is all Orient :

e

" Schéhérazade, depuis mille ans
   Que tu racontes tes balivernes féeriques,
   Ton corps doit être maigre comme une trique,
   Ton nez tout crochu, ta bouche édentée
   Et tes cheveux blancs
   Comme une touffe de lis d'été ;
   Ta peau jadis fraîche comme une pêche
   Doit être jaune comme un parchemin ;
   Tes mains gracieuses, tes fines mains,

     .   .   .   .   .   .

   Et pourtant, Schéhérazade, je te vois
   Toujours jeune et jolie en mon rêve,
   Et la magie mystérieuse de ta voix
   Me berce tour à tour de tristesse et de joie
Sans que jamais le charme se rompe ou s'achève. . . .

The following poem, translated at the last moment, is from *Schéhérazade* :

THE HAPPY NIGHT.

    Leave the lamp alight ;
    Make the fire flare
    With dying cedar boughs ;
    And twine amid thy hair,
    Sweet maiden mine,
    This flower.

    Leave the casement open
    To the delicate eve,
    So that the irised odour
    Of the orchard's almond-trees
    May enter with the water-jet's sad song.

    And till delicious dawn
    Returns to lay its tender burden

Of rosy laurels at thy casement,
Let me love thee, maiden mine,
Until the circles of thine eyes
Are grown like violets.

The most characteristic note of Klingsor is a
sadness breathing like an almost imperceptible
breeze, as in the following poems from *Le Valet de
Cœur:*

SUR LE PONT-NEUF.

Sur le parapet du Pont-Neuf de Paris
  Qui est si vieux, je m'accoude et je rêve :
  Un soir très doux d'automne s'achève
Dans la musique des causeries.

Je rêve : un bateau-mouche léger file
  Vers Auteuil ou vers Saint-Cloud ;
  Un pêcheur prend un goujon au bout
    De son fil.

Je rêve à celles aux airs menteurs d'amour
  Qui sont passées et passeront
  En fins corsets de guêpes et robes de velours
    Sur le pont.

Je rêve à ceux qu'une infidèle trompait
  Et qui ont quitté désespérés leurs lits
  Pour se jeter dans l'eau jolie
    Du haut du parapet.

Je rêve : dans l'air doré Notre-Dame s'élève
  Et Henri-Quatre sourit seul sur le vieux pont
  Par où belles et galants s'en vont ;
    Je rêve . . .

PLAISIR D'AMOUR.

Plaisir d'amour ne dure qu'un moment,
  Et la rose que vous offrirent ce matin
Des doigts fins de damoiseau tendrement
  Aura ce soir froissé ses habits de satin;
Plaisir d'amour ne dure qu'un moment
  Et ne laisse qu'un souvenir lointain.

Plaisir d'amour ne dure qu'un moment,
  Mignonne, ayez-en plus souci ;
Ne renvoyez pas vos princes charmants
Avec une larme au bout de leurs cils ;
  Plaisir d'amour ne dure qu'un moment :
  Chagrin d'amour aussi.

Klingsor has the light touch and the mediæcvalism (Klingsor was a magician of the middle ages) of the delicate Belgian poet whom he celebrates in a dedication :

"Je viens vers vous, mon cher Elskamp,
  Comme un pauvre varlet de cœur et de joie
Vient vers le beau seigneur qui campe
  Sous sa tente d'azur et de soie . . ."

The women poets of France ought to have an anthology all to themselves. (But Mrs. Grundy would make a fuss). Besides the Countess de Noailles and Gérard d'Houville, it would have to include, as stars of the first magnitude, Lucie Delarue-Mardrus, Marie Dauguet, Renée Vivien, and Hélène Picard. These poetesses are at one with those of Germany. They reveal woman. To read their works is like being Paris with the goddesses taking their veils off before one. What English poetess would dare to write such a fine poem as Lucie Delarue-Mardrus wrote in "Refusal"[1] (to be a mother)? Everyone, says this poetess, "porte son sexe ainsi qu'une bête cachée." But the women poets of France turn this beast to the light, as they have a perfect right to do, if living poetry comes of it.

Of Renée Vivien one dare not speak. She was an Anglo-American, born in the United States in 1877. Her love-poems, which are exquisite, are addressed to women. She was the re-incarnation of Sappho.

But one may speak at greater length of Hélène Picard (1878-——), not because she has been praised by Professor Faguet and crowned by the *Académie française*, but because her work, in spite of its audaciousness (she is probably not conscious that it is audacious) is absolutely healthy, and, in the best sense of the term, chaste. Her first book, *L'Instant Éternel*, begins with "Le Poème de la jeune Fille," surely the most illuminating song of virginity that has ever been written :

> "Elle mettra sa robe blanche . . .
> Et posera, pour l'embaumer,
> Une verveine sur sa hanche,
> Car il lui faut un bien-aimé . . ."

One or two poems will give some idea of the charm of this book :

---

[1] *Horizons*, Fasquelle.

LE TROUBLE.

Ah ! laissez-moi bercer mon ineffable rêve,
Je sens d'un autre lin se vêtir ma beauté,
Et la lune est ainsi qu'une averse d'été,
Et la colombe au bord de son nid se soulève . . .

Il semble que je vis dans un biblique jour,
Mes cheveux sont pareils aux vapeurs du cinname,
C'est l'âme de Sion qui chante dans mon âme,
J'ai brûlé des parfums et respiré l'amour.

J'ai crié vers les bois pour réveiller les roses
Et pour en obtenir le cœur du bien-aimé . . .
J'ai compris, en passant dans le vent enflammé,
Que le désir est mûr sur mes lèvres écloses.

Mon rire était ainsi que du cristal brisé,
J'ai supplié la vie en pleurant sur la terre,
Aux arbres, aux ruisseaux, à l'ombre solitaire,
J'ai demandé tout bas le secret du baiser . . .

Le printemps regardait se balancer les cloches,
Toute l'odeur de Pâque était sur les chemins,
Les muguets ont loué la blancheur de mes mains,
Et j'ai su que les temps de mes noces sont proches.

Je veux seule, ce soir, sangloter dans l'air doux,
Oh ! c'est trop de bonheur, trop d'ardeur, trop d'alarmes,
Mes yeux sont étonnés de leurs nouvelles larmes,
Vous ne pouvez savoir encor . . .
                                    Éloignez-vous . . .

LE DÉSIR D'AIMER.

Le désir d'aimer passe sur ma lèvre,
        L'amour est si fort . . .
Je sens dans ma chair de flamme et de fièvre
        Mille aiguillons d'or . . .

Oui, les longs baisers au long souffle tiède,
        Et le frisson fou,
Tout ce qui veut bien, tout ce qui possède,
        Tout ce qui veut tout.

Pleurer d'infini sous la nuit immense,
        Trembler de bonheur,
Mourir de chagrin, d'ardeur, de silence
        Et d'avoir un cœur . . .

Oh ! le Bien-aimé qu'on attend dans l'ombre,
        O soirs inconnus ! . . .
Le désir qui croît, le vouloir qui sombre
        Entre des bras nus . . .

Et le beau courroux et la belle fièvre
        Aux brûlants yeux d'or,
Et la douce lèvre et la douce lèvre . . .
        L'amour est si fort . . .

" L'Instant Éternel" is the heart's story: first virgin longings; then love:

"Oui, quand je vous ai vu, je suis harmonieuse,
Je suis lourde, parée, éclatante, soyeuse,
Riche comme un fuseau chargé de jeune lin.
J'ai le grand désir d'être et de manger du pain,
De m'abattre au milieu d'une épaisseur de roses
Et de tout vous donner à mes paupières closes . . .

Ah ! je suis ivre ainsi que tous les raisins noirs,
Plus pesante d'odeurs que la robe des soirs . . ."

and in her following book, *Les Fresques*, she sings songs of marriage.

Probably Jean de Gourmont goes too far when he says that *all* true poetry is sensual, and even

sexual.[1] That is not true of English poetry:
English poets have found it possible to write
poetry with their brains and not with their genitals.
(Of course the French critic might urge: Is that
true poetry?) But the statement is partly true
of contemporary French poetry, and especially of
that part of it which is written by women. The
Countess de Noailles, Marie Dauguet, and some
other French poétesses might be classed as
"bucolic" poets; but the term would be mislead-
ing. It is true that they know nature intimately,
and they re-create Francis Jammes; but they talk
to nature just as they would talk to a lover. They
identify themselves with nature, they lose them-
selves in it, just as a woman who loves wildly loses
herself in her lover. Take this passage from
Hélène Picard:

> " On pleure, lentement, son âme dans son[2] âme,
> Et l'on est une pauvre, une si pauvre femme . . .
> Et puis, on vole, on croit, on s'enivre, on s'enfuit,
> Dans ses bras étoilés on enferme la nuit.
> On se mêle au nuage, à la forêt, à l'onde,
> On sent battre en sa chair les artères du monde,
> On est arbre, on est fleur, on est terre, on est dieu,
> A pleine soif, on boit des coupes de ciel bleu . . .
> Après avoir tremblé, frissonné de la sorte,
> Et possédé la vie, et le rêve, et la mort,
> Et fait plier ta hanche au poids d'un tel trésor,
> O femme, si l'aimé ne t'aime pas, qu'importe ! . . ."

---

[1] " On peut constater que toute vraie poésie est sensuelle
et même sexuelle: expression d'un état de désir physique,
transposé, elle éveille en nous les images qui l'ont fait
naître."—*Muses d'aujourd'hui*, p. 19.

[2] The lover's.

This pantheism is nowhere more passionate and beautiful than in the verse of Marie Dauguet (1860-—), a poetess who lives in the Vosges mountains.   From such a line as :

"Une odeur de bétail veloute l'air du soir,"

one might know that she had lived at the heart of nature all her life.   But is it nature or feminine surrender which sings in such lines as these :

"Et des taillis tout dégouttants d'humilité
Montaient aux lèvres une odeur de nudité."

Or in this apostrophe to the sea:

"Prends-moi, je suis à toi, voici mes bras ouverts
Et mon corps étendu sur ta couche de sable
A tes baisers trop lourds intensément offerts."[1]

There is a masculine violence in her verse:

"Aimons le tendre Avril ouvrant les primevères
De ses baisers déments ;
Aimons l'été si lourd qui pèse sur la terre
Ainsi qu'nn corps d'amant ;

L'automne sensuel et trouble qni chancelle
Des grappes dans les mains,
Et qui meurtrit les cœurs en ses paumes cruelles
Comme il fait des raisins.

.   .   .   .

---

[1] *Clartés*, Sansot.

Aimons tout de la vie, adorons jusqu'aux larmes
    L'amour mystérieux,
Obéissons au rite où le désir s'acharne,
    Comme au geste d'un dieu.

Ne soyons plus celui qui recule et se cache
    Et, d'avance vaincu,
Craint d'aimer, de souffrir, de créer : c'est un lâche,
    Il n'aura point vécu."

There is a famous sonnet of Verhaeren's which
paints pigs rooting up a muck-heap, while the sun
makes the liquid on their flanks shine like roses.
Marie Dauguet can be equally realistic:

AURORE.

Dans l'étable nuiteuse encor les bœufs s'ébrouent,
Etirent lourdement leurs membres engourdis,
Réveillés tout à coup par un coq qui s'enroue
Et dont le cri strident semble un poignard brandi ;

Trempé d'aube, dehors, le fumier resplendit
Contre un mur délabré qu'une lucarne troue,
Parmi des bois pourris, des socs, des vieilles roues,
Et lance vers le ciel des parfums attiédis.

Cernant une écurie ouverte au toit de mousse,
Qu'emplit un vibrement nuageux d'ombre rousse,
Du purin, noir brocard, s'étale lamé d'or,

Où fouillent du groin activement les porcs,
Et dans la paille humide et qu'ils ont labourée
Le soleil largement vautre sa chair pourprée.[1]

---

[1] *Par l'Amour*, Mercure, 1906.

Of her last book (*Les Pastorales*, Sansot, 1911)
Jean de Gourmont says: "La poétesse ne s'élance
pas vers la nature, elle s'ouvre à elle, avec le désir
d'être violentée par son mystère." "Evening
seizes her," he says, "like an embrace":

> "Tout s'émeut.   On entend l'horizon haleter,
>   La terre sensuelle et lourde palpiter,
>   Que l'émoi des pollens féconds enthousiasme.
>   Ma lèvre est appuyée à la lèvre des dieux,
>   Tout s'épanche, invincible, envahissant les cieux,
>   Une odeur de baisers, d'étreintes et de spasmes."

Movements and manifestos succeed each other
in France. A school becomes decrepit; the young
bloods who first blazoned its programme become,
in their turn, "chers maîtres," rich (for poetry, not
being gagged, pays in France), petted, spoilt,
engrossed by social engagements; and while they
rest on their laurels a new generation raises the
standard of revolt, and flaunts the same flaming
extravagance as their elders did in their green
days.   Symbolism, which killed Parnassianism,
which killed Romanticism, which killed starched
inanity on stilts, is not, as a *genre tranché*, quite
dead yet; nor did the absurd counter-movements
of the *Ecole romane, Humanism, Integralism*, etc.,
weaken it; but there is, at this moment, a new
manifestation which, while not entirely hostile to
symbolism (indeed dutiful and grateful to it in
many respects), is yet in substance an absolutely
different thing, and uses metres which are a further
development of the *vers libre*.   This is the work

of the school of poets known as "le groupe de l'Abbaye."

In no connection whatever with this group stands André Spire. He is a man of ripe years, while the Abbey poets are all flamboyant boys. And yet he has so many points of contact with them that one is tempted to range him along with them.

He is full of the spirit of Nietzsche, but his cult is that of the body more than of the brain. In this he is nearer to Walt Whitman than the cerebral Abbey group. In *Vers les Routes absurdes* he sings:

> "Ah ! j'aimerais aimer, dans ce froid enivrant,
> Un beau corps, exalté d'espace et de vitesse,
> Avec des cheveux pleins de vent ;
> Un beau corps, qui s'agenouille devant lui-même,
> Et qui soit fier, et qui soit arrogant, et qui soit dur.
>
> Ah ! j'aimerais aimer une femme entraînée,
> Dont les solides pieds sachent dire aux montagnes
> Je suis chez moi, chez vous.
> Une femme, qui soit autre chose qu'un sexe
> Que le maître garde au logis pour la caresse.
> Une femme qui choisisse et son jour et son heure,
> Et qu'il faille poursuivre, et de haute lutte
> Prendre.
> Et qui soit mon égale, enfin !"

His rhythms have a phonetic basis, for he is a practical phonetician, and has worked in the laboratory of the Abbé Rousselot. He is a Socialist, a tribune of the people, mourning the tragic things of their life:

"J'ai vu des corps d'enfants guettés par des vieillards,
J'ai vu le ventre las des prostituées lentes ;
J'ai vu des conquérants, des nains et des joueurs,
Des avares, des fous, des pauvres, des esclaves,
Et j'ai pleuré . . ."

It was René Arcos who, in 1907, founded the phalanstery called "The Abbey." Other phalansterians are Georges Duhamel, Jules Romains, and Charles Vildrac. There were also painters, musicians, and sculptors. The Abbey was situated at Créteil, a hamlet twenty kilometres distant from Paris. The old building was the heart of a great romantic park which had been growing hirsute for seven luxuriant years. All weeds, all shrubs, all saplings flourished greenly in touching confraternity. The artists had installed a printing-press in their abode, and they intended to earn their livelihood by publishing the works of art they printed with their own hands. In 1908 they published what future times will perhaps regard as one of the first great poems of the twentieth century: *La Vie Unanime*, by Jules Romains.

The Abbey lasted fourteen months. The material results were disastrous. The expenses were relatively considerable—the profits, nil. The enterprise had to be abandoned. The phalansterians deliberated whether they should blow themselves into the air together with the house, but they could not come to a decision. The "abbatiaux" cherish a tenacious memory of the last winter, which was heroic.

The moral results were appreciable. There was

much derision, but also some interest shown in these young artists who had attempted to live as free men, artists and artisans at once. And they are still banded together, fighting for common ideals of art. They have numerous affinities; but each one strives (keeping that individualism which distinguished the symbolists) to express his personal vision of the world.

After hesitation, investigation, and an intermittent use of the *vers libre* and the classical alexandrine, they have all rallied round the *vers libre*, though each of them tries to institute a personal rhythm.

In absolute contradiction to the partisans of "l'art local" (Heimatskunst), they demand an art of universal significance. Like Alfred Mombert in Germany, they are "cosmic impressionists." The earth is only a province of the world, humanity is one long, lasting cry. They dare to say, proudly, that the aim of the monist world is: lyric emotion! For them, the poet is the beautiful, powerful voice which raises all foreheads heavenwards, dilates chests, and leads the universal chorus. They do not believe in God, they do not believe in gods, but they are drunk with divinity. The poet's mission is to point out the vestiges of divinity.

Jules Romains has written a long poem on "Le Métropolitain"[1] (as "the Tube" is called in Paris). It holds one breathless. In this poet at all events we have something absolutely new.

The year 1910 has brought several new poets to

---

[1] *Deux Poèmes*, Mercure de France, 1910.

the fore.   Edmond Rocher's *Le Manteau du Passé* is a good book.   Here is a poem culled from it:

LOVE THEM ALL.

Desire no single woman: love them all,
But not their soul that is a wile, a gem,
A flower, a furling ribbon ; nor for them
Send out thy soul in quest beyond recall.
Force them with love that to their body clings,
And winds around those swollen fruits of theirs,
And to that soft and curving shell repairs,
The source of joy whence all thy sorrow springs.
Yea, love them for their burning tresses' sake,
And for their deep eyes melting with desire . . .
Women are flowers risen fair from mire,
Which our austere delight may stoop to break.
They fill thy life with sorrows ever fresh;
They are Eternal Beauty passing through
Thy visions ; they are flaring torches who
Illume thee—and the miseries of thy flesh.

A fitting conclusion to this anthology would be an extract from another book published in 1910, Edmond Gojon's *Le Visage penché* (Fasquelle). He has a poem called "The Voice of the Men of To-day":

" Now, while the time to future dawnings races,
    We hail the rising sun with triumph wild ;
Rocked by the wind that beats our iron braces
    More brittle than the playthings of a child.

.   .   .   .

Gods we will be, still higher, higher flying,
    And winnow space until the welkin pants,
Until the globe of earth beneath us lying
    Looks like a pendent apple swarmed with ants.

Our flight, that fain would soar from us, we master;
   Squatting in high Heaven, to our engine pinned,
We hear our motor's heart beat fast and faster,
   And in our canvas swallowed is the wind.

.   .   .   .   .   .

And, still to further victories aspiring,
   With cages as of reeds the skies we scale;
Laden with feelers and with screws, untiring
   Like birds through oceans of the air we sail.

.   .   .   .   .   .

Then, while long cries of triumph hail the taming
   Of the inviolate air by stubborn mind,
Our victory is once again proclaiming
   The majesty of earth and of mankind."

France decaying? France is seething with youth.
Listen to the burthen of another 1910 poem (Pascal
Bonetti's *Les Orgueils*, Sansot):

". . . Comme les aigles
Qui vont de sommet en sommet,
   Ivre d'azur, ivre d'espace,
Moi, l'amant des fauves étés,
Sans m'y salir, toujours je passe
Devant les bouges des cités.
   Ohé! Chantons! La plaine est large,
Le soleil rit dans le matin.
Mes lourds souliers battent la charge
Sur la grand' route du destin."

J. BITHELL.

March 1912.

NOTE.

THE publishers and the translator are grateful to the French poets and their publishers for their generous authorizations to publish these translations of copyright poems. Special thanks must be given to Monsieur Alfred Vallette, the Director of the *Mercure de France*, who owns nearly all the best poetry published in France during the last twenty-five years; but for his assistance it would not have been possible to publish either this volume or its companion, *Contemporary Belgian Poetry*.

Verlaine is not included, because a volume in the "Canterbury Poets" Series is already devoted to him. Tristan Corbière, essentially a contemporary poet in spite of his date, I have found untranslatable. I had obtained authorizations to translate Maurice Magre and Renée Vivien; but, though I admire both, I have, in the end, thought it best to reserve my translations of their work for private circulation. For other Bowdlerizations and deletions the publishers and their editor are responsible.

As to the spirit which has moved my selection, let me quote from Synge's Preface to his *Poems and Translations*, to me the most vital thing in recent English criticism:

"... *the strong things of life are needed in poetry also, to show that what is exalted, or tender, is not made by feeble blood. It may almost be said that before verse can be human again it must learn to be brutal.*"

J. B.

CORRECTIONS.

p. 134, l. 15, my, *read* thy.
p. 148, l. 15, wooden, *read* wooded.

Contemporary French Poetry.

RENÉ ARCOS.
1881-—.

THE GROWTH OF THE GOD.

BURNING gold, and light ;
by the same token : trumpet flourishes !
Plenary joy
to the profit of oblivion.
But better far, the tints of shade :

the life of lines in silence,
one's woman's eyes and their farewells,
serenity's full, speechless sun,
grace inclining, grace and tears,
all that beguiles,
then honey, and absinthe also.

Instants drowned in dream,
thought that dies, but lengthens as it dies,
sister of sighs,
And the delight when dream has built.

If the mind is lucid, and can build the mighty love,
even unto swooning,

a lifted look, a settling hand,
and the whole edifice falls in an avalanche.

Between his birth and death, a man on earth,
amid the mighty coveting and all the powers,
raising more high with every day his cup of soul,
if he can bear the question further, before all,
and make a frontier recede, '
may say : I was the growth of a god.

THE GOD.

IF thou art a collecting-place,
a place in space where all things
are wont to meet
for knowledge and to fructify,
living a heart's offensive life,.
if thou hast taken to thee all ideas,
those, young, which step together like a thousand
        men
clashing cymbals,
and those which, undecided yet, are lost
in those which are serene and spread themselves
like streams in time,

that also which a man who lived alone abandoned,
so great that it obstructs our highest doors,
so tragic, great, and heavy on our shoulders
that none of us has had the strength to move it yet,

if thou hast known all shocks and impulses,
all looks, all coveting of hands,
contagion of fire, and blood, and words,

and if sometimes thou sawest, lighting all men's eyes,
the crown emblazoned high on standards
in clash of weapons, in a rocket of cries,

if thou art centre unto vortices
whereinto rush pell-mell,
rejoicing endlessly because they blend with thine,
the world's pulsations,
if thou sufficest to be all at once,
all that is, and stirs, and strives to be,
if he who is thyself and truest of all
adds to all this
desire still to be more,
desire born of thyself, of him who commands
all strangers come from vasts of space
for the communion of thy mind and blood,
and to shake themselves unto thy semblance,

if thou sufficest to be thus sometimes,
this present a vast future rumbles in,
O thou who art come already from all the dead,
and if, from being so much,
thou movest thyself to the point of being suddenly,
born from thy depths,
the invasion, from stage to stage,
of a strange birth in columns of flames,
to the point of being but this marvellous pang
which digs a vacuum below thy heart,
this laugh, born of thy throat's ecstatic aching,
and if thou wert compelled,
in order from the stifling to be free,
to utter a great cry,
then, at that instant, enjoying in one flash
the swift perception of thy godhead,
thyself shalt be the god.

RELIGION.

THE humiliation with love,
the contrition and the haircloth,
but one must be in a state of grace,
one must not know with the forehead.

Fervour ! There have been days when thou hast
      burned,
like an altar on the days of festival
with flaming gold beneath its candle-forest.
Old need of worshipping more high than men.
There have been days when in thy own despite thy
      knees have yielded.

But poor man walking with joined hands, with lips
      that stir,
—and in thine eyes this radiance of the Magi,—
poor man, where wilt thou fall upon thy knees,
for prayer and psalm ?
        In temples
(upon the flags, along the walls,
in the night-lamps, even to the roofs),
abandoned soul is languishing with the absence
of One departed having left no trace . . .

In temples, this weariness !

With what shalt thou fill up this mighty void of love,
poor man come here,
bearing more love than they in legends bore,
to make here, ah ! what furious offering,
and who hast met none but thyself,
iced as it were, and shrivelled ?

Gospels, and tables of the law,
books, so many books !
But your hands are fallen,
your head is shaking,
with incredulity ;
O the powerlessness of the lie,
in spite of the industrious brain,
O the artifice at every base . . .
And no god any longer for the price of a stratagem.

Thou must then—go thy life in quest.   ·
Thou must then—go chewing this inquietude,
under the weight of this dumbness
and this dense solitude ;
for all is groping, strange to all,
for all is only tendency and all is only possible.

And yet : this awakening
still full of sleep, stretching itself.
Level with the slow century, this game of living,
     keen,
This pollen over the hot minute spread.
This masculine motion, all these movements,
for this unlimited design.
All these nativities that none had prophesied.
     All moves.   All is aspiring.
Every man before him has the man that he would be.
A seizing gesture reaches out with time.

     And yet :
the solidarity of the world's presences ;
—wert thou not gazing, with all thine eyes, at the
     stars,

that night of loveliness thy mouth spake love?—
O certainty obscure !
Something is everywhere that none has said.

Thou canst not seize on any of it,
although thy soul desire it, with thine eyes,
nor with thy hands, nor with thy mind ;
thou comest near it and departest from it ;
it is beside thee, thou wilt seize it soon,
thy life stops that it may let it live,
and it is over, it is gone.

Something is everywhere which goes before, which
    grows,
something which fructifies in this thy present.

HENRI BARBUSSE.

1874-—.

THE SEMPSTRESS.

ON the rain a glint of day . . .
   The blue and yellow sun
   Pours on the suburbs one
Beam through the shower's gray.

In the workshop stingy of light
   Sewing she sits in the gloom,
   But she feels, beyond the room,
The rainbow growing bright.

And when it shines without limit
  On the houses dazzled by
  The rain's sweet rays, a shy
Song she hums to hymn it,

Chanting Time's vast expanse,
  The Future vague and bland . . .
  Her eyes smile on her hand,
She believes in her romance.

And in beauty that amazes,
  And peace for the human race,
  She feels herself beyond space,
Her lips to the light she raises.

Workshop whistles are blown.
  Home, with the evening's crape
  Around her wistful shape,
Singing she goes to her own.

Threading by carriage and cart
  The listless wayfarers loud,
  She is alone in the crowd,
Because of the song in her heart.

Full of impossible things,
  Home to her simple repast,
  Wildered with eyes downcast,
While the music hid in her sings.

HENRY BATAILLE.

1872-—.

THE MONTH OF DAMP.

I HAVE been watching through grey window panes
This evening falling . . .   Someone is astray
Along the ditches filled with autumn rains . . .
O wearied wanderer upon thy way
At the dusk hour when shepherds leave the hill,
Hasten !   The doors are closed, no fires burn
In lands where thou returnest sick and chill.
Empty the highroad is, and the lucerne
Sounds far away faint with discouragement . . .
O hasten : the old lumbering carts have blown
Their lanterns out . . .   It is the autumn, bent
And gone to sleep over the cold hearth-stone . . .
Autumn is singing in the dead vine-shoots . . .
It is the hour when corpses on the flood,
Dreamily floating, feel in their white blood
The first cold risen from the river's roots,
And go down to the deep and sheltering mud.

THE FOUNTAIN OF PITY.

WE have our tears.   This is grief's anodyne,
To know that tears a-many are in store.
And hearts did know them faithful, even before
All dreams had faded.   To the first of mine
My wistful mother said : " How many more?"

We have our tears, a mystery that is past
Our fathoming.   Child, how I pity thee
 To see thee waste them foolishly and fast,
And with no fear of drying up the last !
Yet this is worth being guarded zealously !

No, not the flowers, no, not the summer will
So tenderly console us, only they.
They soothed us young, and they console us still,
Faithful and vigilant so many a day ;
And inward weep when eyes no more will fill.

TRAINS.

THE trains dream in the dew for hours outside
The stations, then unmoor, and grate, and glide . . .
I love the wet trains passing through the fields,
Long caravans of all the country yields ;
Those that sleep in the shunting ; and the train
Clad with tarpaulin cloak against the rain . . .
And trains of bullocks bellowing as they pass
The farm where they were born, and sniff its grass . . .
And all grey carriages close shut and warm,
Whose silence glitters through the pelting storm,
With their inscriptions faded, and their cold,
Pale windows . . . the surrendered rest they hold . . .
Their flickering lanterns when the morning comes . . .
And how the sleepy engine puffs and hums ! . . .
A hand runs up the blind, and pulls it back . . .
The hamlet where the grass grows by the track . . .
The suburbs . . . carriages where nothing stirs,
Where you can hear the breath of passengers . . .
The blue-veiled lamps that palpitate . . . the train

That crosses us and tells us of its pain,
While we in corners brood, and wonder why
We hear it still when it has echoed by . . .
And the green halt where you can hear the quails,
With their sad, solitary note . . . and rails
Blocked, while a whistle sounds and buffers clash,
And regular signals through the darkness flash . . .
Mysterious calls we cannot comprehend . . .
And, after being cradled without end
In jolts the listless soul is broken in,
The snorting entrance, with a brazen din,
Of the train bounding onwards as to joys
In the great cities full of buzzing noise ! . . .
And here refracted is the chaste, white beam,
Which led me through the world from dream to dream,
O infinite rails under the moonlight cold,
To whom my heart its bitterness has told
In all the partings unto which it yields . . .

I love the wet trains passing through the fields.

PATERNE BERRICHON.

1855-—.

TO STÉPHANE MALLARMÉ.

IDEAL monument of cordial dreams,
  The Poem, to its mystery's supreme singer,
  Is a miraculous pool where spirits linger
To quench their fiery thirst with diamond gleams.

Sounds, colours, perfumes, forms fuse in a mesh,
   And soar above the hour's bitter base,
   Projecting through the music thrilling space
Processional altars for the song grown flesh.

God, who the man created, he conceives;
And like a flower his architecture heaves
   O'er strophic walls illumed with stained-glass
      words;

And, with his visions brightening the block,
   With more assiduous sculpturing he girds
The style with marble Time shall never shock.

LOVELINESS.

In the blue jersey which her bosom's wealth
   Stretches, a queen of majesty she seems,
   Rich, royal fruit of love my morbid dreams
Compress to suck the acid juice of health;

And like a lake of flesh she lies up-curled
   Upon her bed, that flowering linen shore
   Her milky heavinesses billow o'er,
By lust's hot breezes swollen and unfurled!

And when she passes with soft, rhythmic pace,
Cradling her fluctuating charms, my face
   Is reddened by a stinging shame intense,

And I am full of a corroding thrill,
   And tortured by a sanguine prurience
Which drowns my delicate, anæmic will.

THE ORCHESTRA.

WEEP, O thou pride of fingers deft that slip
   Their shameless caprice in that narrow sheath,
   Whence die this hollow's lilies underneath
Eros's unrelenting, crackling whip,

While in the centre golden groins vibrate,
   And in a womb a noise of silver throbs,
   And, sucking back his breath that stifles, sobs
The ichoglan on whom young Sultans wait;

With violins of the psychopomp to guide,
Through Lesbian skies your fleeting sorrows glide
   In grey flakes unto Sodom's yellow blaze,

To rumble through the prolix radiance lit,
   Hark! by the red trombone Antinous plays,
Hidden, and roaring laughter fit by fit.

GEORGES DUHAMEL.
1884-—.

THE BEGGAR.

YOU cannot gather up my look, which flows
Towards the earth, and which you seek in vain;
Friend, let it weigh down, and yourself be silent,
I have no wish nor strength to look at you.

You come to me, as men come near a hearth,
Frightened by the hush of your domain,
Preyed on by poverty and pain . . .
But, just to-day, I know not what to give you,
I surely cannot give you what you ask.

Then you speak, accuse yourself,
You make your weakness more, you bare yourself
    before me,
Lessen yourself, in hope
That I shall with a word restore your stature,
Make you bound upwards to the height you had,
Console you, and protest,
—With but one word, like a caress,
With but one word, though whispered.—
You shrink, you grovel on the ground,
You say yourself more lamentable than you are,
To force me to bend down and raise you up.
—One does this for the puniest stranger,
I could not fail to do it . . . you are sure?—

. . . You dig your past up with a pitiless hand,
Confessing wrongs that you have done to me
Which I had no idea you had done,
Denying with uneasy, fainting voice,
All your mind's best.

But vainly you are looking for my eyes . . .
I am tired, do you not know it?
O! say no more! for I would give a day of joy
To have the courage, friend, to throw to you
The word which should restore your strength and
    stature.

But, friend, the more your voice shakes and the more
    you lower yourself,
The more the wish of speaking to you flees from me,
And because you are a man, because I love you,
I long to weep at all I hear you say.

WATER.

THIS water hardly keeps a memory of its sources.
In arteries of cement
It has glided dizzy courses
Towards this city which will be its ocean.

—You see emigrants along the docks,
They have this look of beaten cattle.—

Followed by blows of menacing machines,
It has writhed in leaden corsets,
Driven on to the assault of houses,
And pleating its snoring shivers on their spines.
It is so frightfully anonymous,
It has no personal taste,
And nothing intimate it kept
After the reservoirs of Babel.

Now it is here,
In this enamelled vase
Of an improbable ultramarine,
It is here like a dead water with no history;
You feel it never mirrored anything,
You feel that it has run through territories,
And run through fields of salt, and never tasted them;
It is indifferent and sleeps at random,
And knows of nature only the wrong side.

Then, ten little azure jets
Dance in a circle under the vase.
This scarcely looks like fire,
And yet indeed is fire :
—There were mosses as well as oaks,
There were ferns as well as palm-trees,
Warm wind, aromatized by oceans nigh,
And red sun in the sky ;
There was at that time all the forests
Greeting the dawn with their crowns, beyond the
    havens. . .

Surely, but all these things are deeply dead,
And somewhere corpses must be being tormented ;
Therefore ten little azure will-o'-the-wisps
Gossip in a circle under the vase.
This scarcely looks like fire,
It neither has its manners nor attire,
It is a debonair, obedient company
Which slyly lisps,
And falls back in good order when commanded.

Then falls the water into its abyss of sadness.

Sometimes the city whips
Its childish regiment of window-panes ;
The water scarcely trembles, scarcely takes it ill.

And yet a dream encumbers it,
A dream of a pond, at dusk,
With a flock of vapours, like shadows,
That dramatize their spiral play in the dark.

And truly, twisted, on its face,
Phantoms rise from place to place.

Then, a great inquietude invades it :
Someone with insistence strikes the bottom of the
    vase.
Where is it ?   Ah ! if it could but return !
Quickly, return to the springs it came from !
Pass again through the brute hands of machines,
But yet return !

It is too late, a fry of little pearls
Spontaneously at the bottom dawn ;
The vase, which trembles,
Lets them loose by handfuls,
They sail away, and, suddenly, it is the void,
And the short sobs of souls resigned.

Beneath, the memory of the forests of the ancient
    world.
Ah ! yes, ten azure will-o'-the-wisps in a circle
    clamour.

They say, the wicked tongues,
They say the water is singing.
—But the forced virgin does not sing,
It weeps its torture,
And its bad liberty for ever lost.

It knows now that it might have then descended,
Processioning under the poplars' gaze,
And that, in deltas, ocean languishes with waiting
    for this message
Of olden continents forgotten.

What matter if, in tropic countries, sound
The hollow gulfs with sulphur and volcanoes
    bound. . .

This water is the prisoner of things,
And must atone for men.

But of a sudden it has found its pride again,
And climbs, and foams, and presses forward in a
    crowd of heads,
And the vanished thing with the bursten eyes
Is drunk with simulation of a storm.

A GOSPEL.

O HAPPY feelings coming from outside,
You have so deeply driven into my soul,
You give me the illusion
Of that interior joy
Which wells out of the source within itself.

O happy feelings coming from afar,
You have so wholly lost your memory
That I am simply joyous
Without considering the reasons thereof.

O happy feelings I have used,
Resume your course,
Bear otherwhere your salutation,
Torch that must still endure a little while.
Go, and in other places kindle fires,
My breath is powerful, I shall do the rest.
Go and burn elsewhere, I await it as a signal.

  .   .   .   .   .   .   -

O joy ! art thou so young and natural,
That thy sole hope, or memory,
Or sight of thee in others hides
The highest reasons to be suffering !

2

Joy ! art thou so tenacious and so keen
That even cut down and taken from thy soil
Thou yet canst bloom, disdainful,
And far from all exiled subsist?
—O green laugh of an island on the sea.

O Joy ! like greater grief
Thou fillest the frame and drivest sleep away.
Thou hast seemed to me like a divine possession,
And I shall not be always fit for thee.

I ask, coward as I am, a little pain,
A grief to trail, as men trail their sick foot,
A grief to bear, like mourning for a time,
I crave a sore upon my flank
Through which to bleed, like overflowing health,
All the excess of joy I can no more contain.

PAUL FORT.

1872----.

BEFORE HER WEDDING-DAY.

THIS maiden she is dead, is dead before her wedding-
    day.
They lay her in her shroud, her shroud as white as
    flowering may.
They bear her to the earth, the earth, while yet the
    dawn is grey.
They lay her all alone, alone down in the chilly clay.
They come back merry, merrily a-singing all the way.

" We too shall have our turn, our turn," a-singing glad
    and gay.
This maiden she is dead, is dead before her wedding-
    day.
They go to till the fields, the fields as they do every day.

A BALLAD OF THE SEASON.

The sea is brown and green, and silver-flecked,
    And roars as mountain-shadowed forests do.
The sky's grey velvet in the wind is checked
    With pleats of pallid azure and deep blue.
A beacon-light is virginally paling
A cloud of barques to all horizons sailing,
And into their black sails the ambushed squall
Shoots silver arrows from his iron bow.

But when the sun is hatted with the squall,
    And blearily above the ocean leers,
And when the cliff casts down the autumn's pall
    Which, laughing, weeping, to the sun careers,
Thou, poet-fisherman, dost haste to bring
To the earth's shelter all thy mesh of string,
And waitest, dreaming, for the sovran cloud
To draw the rainbow from its velvet shroud.

A BALLAD OF THE NIGHT.

The maidens short of stature, brown of hands,
With sickles hanging from their arms like moons,
Are drinking air from night's star-studded bowl,
And wending homewards from the woods at gloam.

And when one hums another's answer comes,
And others hum, the humming goes along . . .
Can it be death wafted on ancient song?
The flickering birth of some new, radiant song?

As might a woof of mosses soft and dense,
The scented shade the deep path overbrims,
And o'er brown fields and shining bushes swims.
The shadow is like wadding under feet,
And souls uncages in deliverance, whence
Arises in the air this delicate sound
Of souls that seek each other all around,
And rob the flowers of instinct and of sense. . . .

Less dense the shadow is . . . and now is none ! . . .
The moon's blue cheeks caress cheeks brown with sun,
The teeth are silvered whence this humming comes,
And silvered are the sickles hung from arms
And all that shines, and tinkles sweet, and hums,
It seems as it might be the delicate shiver,
The tender rustling of the stars' blue river,
Strayed from the ether into this deep path.

THE GATHERING OF THE STAR.

UNTO thee shall be given a boat, and thou shalt all alone
    embark . . .
The oars shall sleep along thy slumber in the dark.
And yet the river in the night shall guide.

The river has no way except its own to glide.
Thou shalt discover ocean dwelling with the night at
    hand.
Then strain upon thine oars towards thy star,

Furrowing the sea with furrow straight and far,
As in the sky its rigid pathway burns
Thy faithful, thy familiar star that never turns.

Go simply on thy way, and at the tempest mock,
Divide the billows through the tempest-shock,
Go straight to death, whose isle from vapours far
Shines like a moon, the little island where
All the great sky in dew is mirrored bare. . .
Then land, and gather in the grass thy star.

A BALLAD OF THE FIELDS.

THE devil's ruby eyes peer all night long,
A-hunting mice to spit upon his little prong.

IIe kills three hundred thousand in his wrath,
And throws them in the village pond, and lights his
    prong, and stirs the broth,

Which he will make those lovers swallow, who
Think kissing and caressing is the only thing they have
    to do.

And when they vomit on the pond their hearts, he stirs
The gravy with his little fork, and turns the hearts to
    porringers,

And hangs them on his long, green tail
To make a din, a din all night long in the gale.

THE SAILOR'S SONG.

I LOVED the mother, and I loved the daughter. He sails for many a month, does sailor Jack. I loved the mother when I left her; I loved the daughter, too, when I came back.

One woman is as good as any other! When I set sail I had the bloomin' blues. When I came back we all went on the booze. The mother's dead, the daughter is a mother.

A sailor sails for months and months, my dears. Hello, it's time this tar was on the water. Now, mammy, keep a sharp eye on yer daughter. I'm coming back for her in fifteen years.

PAN AND THE CHERRIES.

I RECOGNIZED him by his skips and hops,
And by his hair I knew that he was Pan.
Through sunny avenues he ran,
And leapt for cherries to the red tree-tops.
Upon his fleece were pearling water drops
Like little silver stars. How pure he was!

And this was when my spring was arched with
    blue.

Now, seeing a cherry of a smoother gloss,
He seized it, and bit the kernel from the pulp.
I watched him with great joy . . . I came
    anigh . . .

He spat the kernel straight into my eye.
I ran to kill Pan with my knife !
He stretched his arm out, swirled—
And the whole earth whirled !

Let us adore Pan, god of all the world !

THE NIGHT OF STORM.

Bowed o'er my staff, but raising not my head, I did
not see the lightning flare. O my flock ! I saw the two
green eye-balls of a cat flit in the air.

He is in the lime-trees, mewing. What a gale ! I
hear Pluto, my dog, bark. I hear some one hail me
"Daphnis" in the pasture-land. Has death come to my
house in the deep dark?

There are great shadows coming, round one lantern
shed. Silence. And then a voice—father, your distant
voice: "Amaryllis is dead."

Bleating, all my flock recoil. Pluto is howling at my
feet. I have no longer any flock, and Death is on me:
this is his breath's heat.

Yes, with one flash of lightning heaven has struck two
lilies ! I will go to gather asphodel with Amaryllis.

O my flock, I am dying. The storm bursts. Alas !
alas ! Damon, the drunkard, is telling me under the
lantern : " All things pass. . . ."

THE REEDS AROUND THE POND.

The swallow flees. The twilight falls apace. The
swallow flees, and the hawk follows. The moon is
sparkling on the pond's chill face, and in its image drowns
itself the swallow.

Why should the reeds around the lake behave as though they cared for living or for dying? It is not for the reeds the hawk is crying.—And grief fades like a wrinkle on the wave.

AFTER MANY YEARS.

IVY has covered all the wall. How many hours, how many tears, since once we loved? How many days?

No roses now; ivy has torn the vine. Where is thy soul? . . . Climbing o'er the swallows' nests, the ivy has stifled all the manor.

O wind! The roses of old time have filled the well.— Is it there that thou hast hidden, my dead wife?

None answers. Who should answer? . . . Were it not better listen to the wind singing in the grasses: "My sweet love"?

Level with the roof the ancient sun, the crimson sun, is through the middle cut so sadly.

Shall I call the gardener? The gardener? It would be better call to Death to mow the grass.

So many memories and so much love, and the sun level with the earth.

REMY DE GOURMONT.
1858-—.

HAIR.

THERE is great mystery, Simone,
In the forest of your hair.

It smells of hay, and of the stone
Cattle have been lying on;

Of timber, and of new-baked bread
Brought to be one's breakfast fare;
And of the flowers that have grown
Along a wall abandonèd;
Of leather and of winnowed grain;
Of briers and ivy washed by rain;
You smell of rushes and of ferns
Reaped when day to evening turns;
You smell of withering grasses red
Whose seed is under hedges shed;
You smell of nettles and of broom;
Of milk, and fields in clover-bloom;
You smell of nuts, and fruits that one
Gathers in the ripe season;
And of the willow and the lime
Covered in their flowering time;
You smell of honey, of desire,
You smell of air the noon makes shiver;
You smell of earth and of the river;
You smell of love, you smell of fire.

There is great mystery, Simone,
In the forest of your hair.

FERNAND GREGH.

1873-—.

LOVE'S AWAKENING.

SOMETIMES my hair would brush her rosy cheek,
  Our hands clasped timidly with touch that thrilled,
  Tears trembled in our eye-lids, we were filled
With a strange joy that would not let us speak.

But as in trance we laughed, and silence tense
   Followed, while we were listening to the bees
   Humming among the flowering elder-trees,
A gold noise in the green, warm somnolence.

And then our lips opened to murmur words
   Infinite, which with lips unparted seemed
To sing as with the voice of distant birds,

   And, rising like the echo of things dreamed,
Quivered upon our lips, ecstatic, hot . . .
But we could only smile, and speak them not.

               —*La Maison de l'Enfance.*

IRREPARABLE.

WHAT have we done, my poor, pale dear, alas !
   What was this frantic whirlwind of desire
   That took our souls in kisses, sobs, and fire,
To cast us back half dead upon the grass . . .

What were these throbbing, sobbing, dolorous spasms,
   This hymen that soared with us to the height
   Of burning human bliss, and yet with fright
Seemed to be hovering over cruel chasms?

Alas ! What have we done ? The sun is prying
   Under the boughs, the bees still hum apace,
As when my hands seized yours and would not sever:

Nothing at all is changed, but you are crying . . .
   And I can look no more into your face . . .
Something in us is broken now for ever !

               —*La Maison de l'Enfance.*

THE RUINED TERRACE.

THE ruined steps, half-buried in the ground,
  Moss, and a rose-tree labyrinth invade,
  Whose full-blown blossoms by the wind are swayed,
Whose stems are by dark, quivering ivy bound.

And when our hands touched the old balustrade,
  We found it soft and smooth; and with no sound
  We trod o'er strown rose-petals all around,
Our feet above them glided, half afraid.

And so, a pair that dreamed or sang, we clomb
Never the steps unto that ancient home,
  Save with uncertain feet on stones long crumbling;

And the dwelling seemed a broken heart, with lone
Threshold o'er-run with flowers and ruin-strown,
  Where Joy and Love can only enter stumbling.
                    —*La Maison de l'Enfance.*

AUTUMN FRUIT.

YOUR loved mouth has the sharp and acid smell
Of fruits unripened, although golden-faced.

They tempt the greedy mouth, which cannot tell
Why they, being golden, should so bitter taste.

But soon the lip, accustomed to their scent,
Tastes with their bitterness a sweetness blent.
                    —*La Maison de l'Enfance.*

COURTESANS.

O COURTESANS, Love's witching, wild priestesses,
　　You charm the universe from end to end!
Heroes are always fettered by your tresses,
　　Kings for their pleasure on your bed depend.

Your pose is graceful, and your nostril quivers,
　　Your feet go dancing, and your deep eyes burn,
Your supple bodies bend like reeds of rivers,
　　Your robes like incense round about you turn.

Poor men are full of anger when they see you
　　Come from your segregation of disgrace,
Matrons cast envious eyes at you and flee you,
　　And the wise, scolding, turn away their face.

But still the sighs of boys with passion paling
　　Soar up to you in sultry evenings when
You pass, the dreams of lonely artists trailing,
　　And gray regrets of amorous old men;

And long, strong sighs of young men sick and ailing,
　　Whose blood chafes at the scent the summer floats,
Longing to take your breasts like fruits, inhaling
　　Love in the odour of your petticoats.

—La Beauté de Vivre.

DESIRE.

DAS EWIG WEIBLICHE.

DESIRE rules over men, those half-gods vain,
And is the tyrant of their heart and brain.
He fashions women amorous or chaste,
And when he abdicates, his subjects waste!
The simple souls of little girls and boys
Precociously dream of clandestine joys;
Scarce have we left the paps that reared us first,
A naked breast fills us with fiercer thirst;
And such a keen and secret pleasure preys
On old men mourning far-departed days;
Nay, it may be that in the hour of death
Old spasms echo in the rattling breath,
And withered, icy hands that seek above
The sheets, are moved by memories of love . . .
Desire is our innumerable king
In the earth's womb or spaces wildering.
His long, invisible, gold fetters yoke
The moon to the sea, the agaric to the oak,
And, in blue deeps beyond our vision's bounds,
Make orbs serene blend their melodious sounds;
He calls out of the souls of bards sublime
Their noblest verse, and marries rime with rime;
Yea, everywhere his august force entwines
The elms with vine, and ivy weds to pines.
Desire enlaces life with life!   The crust
Of.earth has for the sun the same dark lust
As in the gamut rote to rote still turns—
The Cosmos for eternal woman yearns!

—Les Clartés humaines.

TO RIMBAUD.

I, WITH my simple fate contented well,
Rimbaud, I love thy mad, incurable,
Bohemian soul, Musset among the tramps,
Dreamer on bridges and by harbour lamps,
Pale sleeper on cold station-benches, stray
Tossed into inns where boils the sudden fray,
Friend of marauding cabmen, nightly rover,
Then of a sudden vagrant eastwards over
Oceans whose bitter spray revived thee, then
Sailing thy *Drunken Boat* unseen of men,
Following thy tranced dream under skies so filled
With noise of voices that thy own was stilled.
Ah ! thy nostalgic heart felt at its core
The poet is a nomad evermore,
The man tormented by the ceaseless thirst
Of draining all sensations, being first
Throughout unknown infinity, still changing
Both soul and scene, and further, further ranging,
Seeking an anodyne for fever-stress,
And the last lurking-place of happiness !

—*La Chaîne éternelle.*

CHARLES GUÉRIN.

1873-1907.

FAIN WOULD I BE A MAN.

FAIN would I be a man ; now in no wise
My poems answer man's distress and cries.

Some men will wile their idleness away
With them, as in a sumptuous café
In pleasured peace they listen for a time
To music sweetly veiling thought and rime.
The sad will seek no consolation here,
Women will be indifferent, and the sneer
From cynics' bitter lips is sure to fall:
" Words, words, for ever words, and that is all.
This is a child crying ere it is hurt,
A mountebank in mimicry expert . . .
What call has *he* to moan of amorous woes,
He with his flute and sonnet-furbelows,
He who with wreaths of patient, polished lines
The marble of his little griefs entwines !"
Ladies and gentlemen, alas, 'tis true !
Give me the bitter genius I should need
To reach your hidden hearts, and make them bleed !
O I were fain if I could offer you
A book that lovers would for love's sake keep,
And since there are but words, O that I knew
At least the magic words that make men weep.

PARTINGS.

O TRAGIC hours when lovers leave each other !
Then every mistress feels herself a mother,
And, making of her lap a chair of ease,
Cradles us in the hollow of her knees,
And turns aside her brimful, dreaming eyes,
And with brief voice to our vain vows replies,
And hums a tune, and whispers, and at whiles
Smooths with slow, gliding hand our hair, and smiles
As laughs a babe to angels over him.

In her strange eyes her heart's dark sorrows swim;
Convulsively her arms strain us to her;
She moans and trembles, and, with sudden stir,
Presses her lips upon our eyes, and bids
Silence, and drinks our soul through closed eye-lids.

VAIN VOWS.

THIS winter night is odorous of spring.
Dreaming, my casement open wide I fling.
Upon a veil of silk the wind seems flying.
A dog barks, and the scented pines are sighing.
The silence is an urn that every noise
Falls into. O my heart yearns for the joys
Of those who in this tender night-hour fling
Their casements open to this whiff of spring,
And gaze up to the sky, and, drinking space,
Taste all infinity while they embrace.
Their drunken souls soar to the stars in flight:
"How beautiful," they breathe, "is life to-night!"
And the wind wafts caresses o'er their hair.

Sweet melancholy of a loving pair,
Wherein the virgin whom her lover strains
Yields like a lily overwhelmed with rains!
Such melancholy I remember well
And bitterly, and the firm vows that fell
From lips that sealed my own. With a slow wing
The gentle night was o'er us hovering.
My darling, you were sighing, tired I was.
And we were silent, love spoke long. Alas!

THE BRIDAL NIGHT.

BRIDEGROOM and bride, with hearts like a wild song,
Sit in the cushioned carriage all day long;
Already they caress their dream, and smile
What lips were loth to speak for yet a while;
And sometimes, too, the sweet and tender things
Said in their hands' and knees' mute parleyings
Call to their faces all their hearts' hot blood.
The train threads scenes that noble mansions stud,
But all that each sees of the earth and skies
Is what is mirrored in the other's eyes.
The day falls, and the cottages of dales
Are lit at mountains' feet that vapour veils.
Now in the west they see a star, the bright,
Propitious omen of the bridal night.
They hear the rails under the carriage groan,
Sparks from the engine through the dark are blown;
They pull the lamp's blue curtain down, and so,
Enlaced, fall half asleep before they know.

Time runs.   But suddenly they feel the shine,
Through eye-lids closed, confused, of lamps in line.
Arrival.   To an ivied inn they go,
With balconies o'erhung by gables low.
The bridal-chamber has been ready made;
Dark is it, but a window in the shade
Gleams like a dazzling frame filled by the moon.
There with caressing arm, and words that croon,
The bridegroom leads the dream-enchanted girl
To see the mountain lake shine like a pearl.
Seeking the farther shore of it they peer,
And hear the lapping of the short waves near,
And vessels of the port that drag their chains,

And blend their rhythm with orchestra strains
Cast down the mountain from some glacier's inn.
Trains rattle through the rocks with rumbling din,
And, while they hear their thunder fade, they see
The lime-leaves shivering on the lonely quay.

.   .   .   .

But now they turn, and, with their fever weak,
The nuptial whiteness of the bed they seek.

.   "   .   .   .   .   .

TO FRANCIS JAMMES.

O JAMMES, your house is like your face.   A beard
Of ivy overgrows it, and a pine
Shades it, as young for ever as your heart,
Spite of the wind and winters, and of grief.
The low wall of your yard is gilt with moss,
The house has but one humble storey, grass
Grows round your garden well and laurel-tree.
When like a dying bird I heard your gate
Cry, warm emotion made my spirit faint.
Long had my feet been borne towards you, Jammes,
And you were as my dreams had pictured you.
I saw your dogs lolling along the road,
And your frank eyes with melancholy smiling
Under your magpie hat of black and white.
Your pensive window sees the land meet sky,
Here are your pipes, and in your book-case glass
The fields reflected over poets' books.

Since they were born, books will grow old, dear friend,
Others will laugh at what has made us weep.
But let not either of us, spite of age,
Forget the day when firmly we clasped hands,
A day as mild as when the autumn wanes,

We heard the tomtits singing in the hedge,
The bells were humming, carriages passed by . . .
It was a sad and long Palm Sunday: you,
Broken o'er love like a reed o'er water which
Trembles and under the wave sobs secretly,
I, quivering, keen to die of the departure
Upon that sea where barques turn pilotless.
We heard the tinkling bells of waggonettes,
Equally both were stirred by different thoughts,
And the grey heaven weighed on our wounded souls.
Shall I come back to sleep in your child's room,
Shall I come back with lashes wind-caressed,
To wait for the first star beneath your shed,
And in your little rose-wood coffer breathe,
Among the yellow heap of old, closed letters,
Love that alone survives in ash of things?
Jammes, he who leans out of your window sees
Villas, and fields, the verge, and mountain snows;
In May you murmur verses in your porch,
The sky's blue fills the gutters of your roof . . .
Melodious home, my friend, shall I return?

To-morrow?   Rather think of yesterday.
A homeless soul is cabined in my frame.
This was of all the heavy evenings I
Have e'er endured one of the heaviest:
The setting sun lavished its splendour o'er
The sea, and gilded all the marge of sand
Where I with brine-drenched air walked on and on,
Rolled like a pebble by the force of dreams,
With the deafening din of billows calling me,
Voice of volcanic, torrid lands and isles.
And full of you my heart has with a pebble,
Veined like a virgin's arm and white as milk,
Marked the day spent with you, Virgilian!

THE JOURNEY'S END.

AT the road's end
The sun goes down;
Give me your hand,
And give me your mouth.

This spring is as black
As a faithless heart;
I am thirsty, give me
Your tears to drink.

O dusk from above!
The angelus rings;
Give me the love
That your breasts tremble with.

The road descends,
White ribbon of leagues,
The last, long slope
Of the blue hills.

Now stay, and look
At yonder trees,
And the smoking roofs
Where a village dreams:

For I will there
In the porchways sleep,
Among your hair
Full of withered leaves.

THE DELICATE EVENING.

THE delicate evening, with its clear, blue mist,
Dies like a word of love on summer's lips,
Or like the wet, warm smile of widows, who
Dream in their flesh of olden bridal joys.
The city far away has hushed its noise ;
In the grave garden where the silence blooms '
The warm, nocturnal wind discreetly sprays
The fountain freshness o'er the gravelled ways,
O'er which like rustling foliage dresses trail ;
The hum of wasps sounds low, and roses, shed
By thoughtful fingers, languorously spread
Their soul of honey stirring love ; a pale,
Strange dawn roves round the confines of the sky,
And blends in mystic, immaterial charm
The fleeing radiance with the starry dark.

What share in all the suns to be have I,
In love, youth, genius, gold, and fiery strife ! . . .
O let me fall into a long sleep now,
Sleep, with a woman's hands upon my brow :
And close the window opened there on life !

A.-FERDINAND HEROLD.
1865-—.

SNOW IS FALLING.

SNOW is falling on the ground,
Shadows on the ground are falling.

Leaves are whirled beyond recalling,
The withered leaves are dead also,
Snow and shadows fall around.

It is as though dread angels knocked
The rusty knockers of the doors fast locked,
Angels slaying us with ailings slow.

And on the verge sad clouds are trailing . . .

All the houses are closed like sombre tombs,
Slow snow is filling all the gathered glooms.

MAROZIA.

UPON the terrace where the shadow falls,
Engarlanded by vines with golden grapes,
Marozia, whom a thin gown scantly drapes,
Sits with her cousin dukes and cardinals.

A chosen troupe of slaves before her dance,
Daughters of Emirs that adore Mahound ;
And poets sing her madrigals, whose sound
Lulls her into a dreamful, amorous trance.

And never with rude wing bird of the night
Hath brushed her maiden brow in ominous flight,
And never lover's love for her grew cold.

The Pope for her would empty treasure-ships,
And clerks and kings would die with singing lips
For one glance of her broad eyes sown with gold.

BERTILLA.

THE Abbess on the psalter's parchment rim
Is painting doves and griffins met in love ;
And ivy twined with olive, and, above,
Against the azure sky flit cherubim.

She paints the Babe asleep in straw, the glad
Shepherds with carven crooks, and the three Kings
Whom from the radiant East the star y-ladde,
With frankincense and golden offerings.

Sweet reveries paints she with her pious hand,
Grave John the Baptist thin in ragged locks,
And in the daisied, mystic meadow-land
Stands the Good Shepherd keeping his chaste flocks.

And Christ's gashed head bends from the wall to
  bless
The cunning painting of the good Abbess.

AUTUMN.

DEAR, do you see the autumn fruits a-lying?
Listen, what slow, monotonous flute is sighing
A song of parting through the shivering wold?
O the song of the flute is pale, the tune so old
Its passing seems to wither all the leaves.
The sky has lost now its diaphanous eves
Which charmed your eyes not very long ago.
No gladioli now nor lilies blow,
And see the rose-leaves on the garden grass,
The last flower that the autumn slays, alas!
Dear, can you hear the falling of the fruit?
Into the night sounds, weeps the woodland flute,
Into the night that veils our happy path,
Into the night that all things shadowed hath.

GÉRARD D'HOUVILLE.

PSYCHE.

NOISELESSLY through the silent mansion treading,
　　She bears a lamp and guards its flickering light ;
Her saffroned veil floats through the green dusk,
　　shedding
　　The perfume of a flower that scents by night.

Noiselessly through the house of dream she paces ;
　　Childlike must be her visage shadowed o'er ;
And her divine leg, pale and slender, places
　　A prudent foot upon the naked floor.

Her knee through her transparent linen presses ;
　　Sometimes her belly glimpses its smooth charm ;
Or else, to heighten her shed auburn tresses,
　　Kindles and rounds itself her supple arm.

Upon her narrow, polished shoulder, binding
　　Her long neck to her hips curved like a bell,
Her airy scarf is ravelling or unwinding
　　The spiral of a great and nacreous shell.

Her hand that guards the frail, rose wick is painted
　　By a pure flame of crimson ; and, as rests
On a dark rose a butterfly half fainted,
　　Her kindled fingers hide her darkling breasts.

Now, as in dread, her curious search she hastens ;
　　No more is seen her hesitating light ;
Her errant beauty, which the darkness chastens,
　　Is lost in the enchanted mansion's night . . .

At dawn returning with a face of paleness,
   She hears her bosom in the silence beat ;
Her veil floats through the irised dawn its frailness,
   And the smooth floor is cold to her bare feet.

For she has seen, on skins of beasts still dreaming,
   Love terrible, mysterious, and grim,
With ready arrows in his clasped fist, seeming
   All bloody in the dusk and lamplight dim.

And she has seen his mouth's inhuman smiling,
   In which his lustful hate and anger stir,
And felt, beside his couch, an unbeguiling
   Invincible, swift horror seize on her.

She flees, the folly of her heart bewailing ;
   Her yellow veil swells in the morn's blue shine ;
Her eyes are frantic, and her strength is failing
   With having seen Love·. . . whom she deemed
     divine !

VISCOUNT ROBERT D'HUMIÈRES.
1868-—.

TO HEDDA GABLER.

Beautiful Queen of the Moderns, logical bloom
   Of feminine fever, who thy brows dost dress
In vine-leaf and dost call on Bacchus whom
   Thou shrinest in thy bleeding heart's recess,

Driven desperate by the tragic ugliness
   Of man, and lust, and day, and the mind's gloom,
Thy anarchist bullet kills with the murderess
   The Future doubled in thy dolorous womb

And from the Promise its fulfilment robs,
When in thy flank that cries for life and throbs
Dies the dread germ.   What Will unknown to thee

Decrees the World's dark for another span ?
Or shall the womb of woman no more be
A certain refuge for the hopes of man?

FRANCIS JAMMES.

1868-—.

I LOVE . . .

I LOVE in old days Clara d'Ellébeuse,
The school-girl of old boarding-schools,
Who, on warm evenings, sat beneath the limes,
Reading the magazines of olden times.

I love but her.   Upon my heart is streaming
The blue light of her white breast.
Where is she now?   Where was this happy nest?
Branches peered into the room where she was dreaming.

It may be possible she is not dead.
Perhaps we both were dead behind those walls.
In the great court-yard withered leaves were shed
In the cold wind of very olden falls.

Those peacock feathers . . . Can you recollect
Their great vase near the sea-shells in a row? . . .
There came news of a ship that had been wrecked
Upon *the Bank*—Newfoundland, as you know.

Come, come to me, dear Clara d'Ellébeuse ;
Let us be lovers yet, if you exist.
In the old garden there are old tulips.
Come quite naked, O Clara d'Ellébeuse.

THE OLD VILLAGE.

The old village was with roses filled,
   And I went wandering in the heat of day,
And, after, o'er the sleeping leaves that chilled
   The feet that walked among them where they lay.

And then along a worn-out wall, the belt
   Of a wide park whence came a gentle breeze,
And there an odour of the past I smelt
   In the white roses and the mighty trees.

Now uninhabited by anyone . . .
   They used to read here when this grass was cropped . . .
   And now, as though the rain had but just stopped,
The ebon-trees shine under the raw sun.

The children of old time went, linking hands,
   In the park's shade, and romped around these roots . . .
   Playing about red plants with dangerous fruits
That had been brought from very distant lands.

Their parents, pointing out the shrubs that thrived
   In the rich soil, would say to them: Take care!
There's poison here . . . from India this arrived . . .
   And that is belladona over there.

They said besides: This tree here by the wall,
   Your uncle brought it with him from Japan . . .
Then it was very delicate and small,
   With leaves as big as the finger-nails of a man.

They said besides: We can remember yet
   The day he came back from the ends of the earth;
He galloped through the village in a sweat,
   With pistols sticking in his saddle-girth.

One summer eve.   The girls ran to and fro
   In the park's shadow round the great tree-stems,
Round the black walnuts where white roses grow,
   And laughter underneath the black yoke-elms.

They shouted: "It is uncle!" seeing him,
   And he, dismounting from his great horse stood
In his great coat and hat with the broad brim . . .
   His mother wept: My son . . . O God is good . . .

We've weathered many and many a storm, he said . . .
   We ran short of fresh water for a week.
   And his old mother kissed him on the cheek,
Saying through tears: My son you are not dead . . .

But where is now this family?   Are these
   But dreams of things that never have existed?
Now there are only shining leaves on trees
   That might be poisoned, they are all so twisted.

Now in the great heat all is hushed and still . . .
And the black walnuts' shadow is so chill . . .
Now uninhabited by anyone . . .
The ebon•trees shine under the raw sun.

THE FOREST PATHS.

THE forest paths are muddy, after the rain ;
The meadows are soaked through and through again,
The blackbirds in the yellow osiers sing,
The yellow osiers good for basketing.
I have been drinking at the rusty spout,
That glints with moss and spits the cold source out.
I would have loved you in this mossy place,
In days gone by, because of your sweet face.
But now I smile, as I my pipe begin,
The dreams I had were like magpies that spin.
I have reflected.   And read novels, then
Verses from Paris, made by clever men.
Ah ! they are far from sources in the rocks,
Where, among withered leaves, bathe brown woodcocks.
They should be here to see the huts I know,
Left ruined in the forest long ago.
And I would show them silver snipe, and thrushes,
Mild-mannered peasants, shining holly-bushes.
Then they would smoke their pipe, smile, and be glad,
And, if they suffer still, for men are sad,
They would be healed much when they heard the noise
Of pointed hawks that over farm-yards poise.

IT IS GOING TO SNOW.

IT is going to snow in a few days. . I remember
   This time last year.   My heart, O how it bled !
   Had I been asked : " What ails thee ? " I should have
      said :
" Nothing.   Leave me alone.   It is December."

O those bad thoughts ! I had no good of them,
  This time last year when heavy snow was cloaking
  The world outside.   And now as then I am smoking
A pipe of briar-wood with an amber stem.

And still my old oak chest of drawers smells good.
  But I was foolish, for these things can never
  Be changed, and they do only pose as clever
Who drive away the things bred in their blood.

Why do we think, and why, like the bees' humming,
  Must these our tongues be talking?   We understand
  Kisses and tears although they speak not, and
Sweeter than sweet words is a comrade's coming.

The stars have been baptized by name and class
  Although they need it not, and figures showing
  That beautiful comets through the darkness going
Will pass through light will force them not to pass.

Where is last year's distress?   My memory fails me,
  What weeds of woe were in this heart full-grown.
  I should answer : " It is nothing.   Leave me alone,"
If someone in my chamber asked : " What ails thee?"

MADAME DE WARENS.

MADAME DE WARENS, you would watch the storm
Folding the dark trees of your sad *Charmettes*,
Or else you played the spinet, in a fret,
You clever woman whom Jean-Jacques would scold.

It may have been an evening such as this . . .
The sky was blighted by black thunder-clouds . . .
The smell of branches cut before the rain
Was sadly from your boxwood borders blown . . .

And I can see him petulant at your knees,
The poet-child, the boy-philosopher . . .
Why in the rosy sunsets would he weep,
And watch the swinging of the magpies' nests?

How he entreated you with heart-felt tears
To put a check on your extravagance . . .
For you were as light-hearted as, alas!
It is the weakness of your sex to be . . .

But you, as bright as you were sweet and tender,
Would say to him : Little philosopher!. . .
Or, laughing, chase him with some rosy drug
With which you powdered him his little wig.

Sweet refuges! Sweet years! O sweet retreats!
The alders whistled fresh among the beeches . . .
The yellow honeysuckle framed the window . . .
A priest would pay a visit now and then . . .

Madame de Warens, you were very fond
Of this young rascal with his eager face,
Slow in his answers, but by no means dull,
Who copied music, too, so cleverly.

Inconstant woman, how you should have wept,
When you forsook him, and he went away
With his poor little bundle o'er his shoulder,
Alone, through pinewoods where the torrents roar . . .

AMSTERDAM.

THE pointed houses lean so you would swear
That they were falling.   Tangled vessel masts
Like leafless branches lean against the sky
Amid a mass of green, and red, and rust,
Red herrings, sheepskins, coal along the quays.

Robinson Crusoe passed through Amsterdam,
(At least I think he did), when he returned
From the green isle shaded with cocoa-trees.
What were the feelings of his heart before
These heavy knockers and these mighty doors ! . . .

Did he look through the window-panes and watch
The clerks who write in ledgers all day long ?
Did tears come in his eyes when he remembered
His parrot, and the heavy parasol
Which shaded him in the sad and clement isle ?

" Glory to thee, good Lord," he would exclaim,
Looking at chests with tulip-painted lids.
But, saddened by the joy of the return,
He must have mourned his kid left in the vines
Alone, and haply on the island dead.

I have imagined this before the shops
Which make you think of Jews who handle scales,
With bony fingers knotted with green rings.
See ! Amsterdam under a shroud of snow
Sleeps in a scent of fog and bitter coal.

Last night the white globes of the lighted inns,
Whence issue heavy women's whistled calls,
Were hanging down like fruits resembling gourds.
Posters blue, red, and green shone on their walls.
The bitter pricking of their sugared beer
Rasped on my tongue and gave my nose the itch.

And in the Jewry where detritus lies,
You smell the raw, cold reek of fresh-caught fish.
The slippery flags are strown with orange-peel.
Some swollen face would open staring eyes,
A wrangling arm moved onions to and fro.

Rebecca, from your little tables you
Were selling sticky sweets, a scanty show. . . .

The sky seemed pouring, like a filthy sea,
A tide of vapour into the canals.
Smoke that one does not see, commercial calm
Rose from the husked roofs and rich table-cloths,
And from the houses' comfort India breathed.

Fain had I been one of those merchant princes,
Who sailed in olden days from Amsterdam
To China, handing over their estate
And home affairs to trusty mandatories.
Like Robinson before a notary
I would have signed my pompous procuration.

Then honesty had piled from day to day
My riches more, and flowered them like a moon-
  beam
Upon my laden ships' imposing prows.
And in my house the nabobs of Bombay
Would have been tempted by my florid spouse.

4

The Mogul would have sent a gold-ringed negro
To traffic, with a smiling row of teeth,
Under his spreading parasol.   And he
Would have enchanted with his savage tales
My eldest girl, to whom he would have given
A robe of rubies cut by cunning slaves.

I should have had my family portrayed
By some poor wretch whose paintings lived and
      breathed :
My plump and sumptuous wife with rosy face,
My sons, whose beauty would have charmed the
      town,
My daughters, with their pure and different grace.

And so to-day, instead of being myself,
I should have been another, visiting
A pompous mansion of old Amsterdam,
Launching my soul before the plain devise,
Under a gable : Here lived Francis Jammes.

PRAYER TO GO TO PARADISE WITH THE ASSES.

O GOD, when You send for me, let it be
Upon some festal day of dusty roads.
I wish, as I did ever here-below
By any road that pleases me, to go
To Paradise, where stars shine all day long.
Taking my stick out on the great highway,
To my dear friends the asses I shall say :
I am Francis Jammes going to Paradise,

For there is no hell where the Lord God dwells.
Come with me, my sweet friends of azure skies,
You poor, dear beasts who whisk off with your ears
Mosquitoes, peevish blows, and buzzing bees . . .

Let me appear before You with these beasts,
Whom I so love because they bow their head
Sweetly, and halting join their little feet
So gently that it makes you pity them.
Let me come followed by their million ears,
By those that carried paniers on their flanks,
And those that dragged the cars of acrobats,
Those that had battered cans upon their backs,
She-asses limping, full as leather-bottles,
And those too that they breech because of blue
And oozing wounds round which the stubborn flies
Gather in swarms.   God, let me come to You
With all these asses into Paradise.
Let angels lead us where your rivers soothe
Their tufted banks, and cherries tremble, smooth
As is the laughing flesh of tender maids.
And let me, where Your perfect peace pervades,
Be like Your asses, bending down above
The heavenly waters through eternity,
To mirror their sweet, humble poverty
In the clear waters of eternal love.

LOVE.

Lass, when they talk of love, laugh in their face.
They find not love who seek it far and wide.
Man is a cold, hard brute.   Your timid grace
Will leave his coarse desires unsatisfied.

He only lies.   And he will leave you lone
Upon your hearth with children to look after,
And you will feel so old when he reels home,
To fill the morning hours with obscene laughter.

Do not believe there is any love for the winning.
But go to the garden where the blue skies pour,
And watch, at the greenest rose-tree's dusky core,
The silver spider living alone, and spinning.

WITH FEET AT THE FIRE.

WITH feet at the fire, I am thinking of those birds
Which told Columbus that the land was nigh.
Water, water, water far as the sky.
At last a sailor shouted out these words :

"Land ! Land !"   The wind sang through the
        ropes.   The crew
Fell on their knees.   They saw beyond gainsaying
The New World's forests with their monkeys blue,
And heavy turtles on the sands were laying.

O when, like a sailor in his gladness crying,
Shall I upon the shore of sunshine leap
Of her hair scattered on her body lying,
Like a new island in the midst of sleep.

THE CRICKET'S SONG.

LAST night the cricket sang when all was still.
I cannot tell you what he sang about.
His singing made the darkness thicker still.
The sad flame of my candle lengthened out.

Well, in the end I had to go to bed,
Telling myself with heavy heart that I
Should ne'er be happier than in days gone by,
And that this song was I, and nothing else.

Child, listen to the cricket's chirping. Thou
Hast nothing save this song to comfort thee.
But understand how deep it is, and how
It fills the heart's dark valley utterly.

Man's pain grows still in the night's silences.
Only the baker-cricket thrills thee through.
Is it a faint complaint to God? And is
The cricket's the one voice God listens to?

Hark what he sings. He sings our hard-earned
    bread,
And in the bitter ashes the cracked pot.
The dog asleep. The housekeeper abed.
Something sad, good, and pure, I know not what.

He says he is my friend. He says, besides,
My farmer wed his bride the other day,
And that the farm was full of love, the bride's
Heart like a blossom-scented cherry-spray.

He says that to the wedding I was fetched,
And that with solemn slowness this young pair
Showed me their room and open bride-bed where
The youngest sister of the bride was stretched.

The wedding-guests have danced and gone away.
The wife lies where her youngest sister lay.
The joy is simple in the hallowed bed.
The clock and cricket in the silence wed.

THE FARMER'S DAUGHTER.

AND the Church bells rang merrily, for they
Rang o'er the farmer's daughter's wedding-day.
The Church rang o'er the glorious August maize,
Rang o'er the dry, red thatch in summer's blaze,
Over the peace of barns rang out the bells,
Rang over sheds and shippons, rang o'er wells
That stirred the silence with their rusty chain,
Rang over corn-lofts heaped with golden grain,
Rang o'er the threshing-engine's puffing snort,
Rang over wenches rosy-cheeked and swart
Running to see the wedding, rang and throbbed
With bridal ecstasies that sang and sobbed,
And rang above the sleepy oxen who
Stopped puzzled, lifting their pale horns unto
Those hearts of the hedge the roses of Bengal.
And tumblers swelled their backs upon the wall,
And, diapered as water is, with their
Spurred, rosy feet cut through the azure air.
And the farmer's daughter, like an opening flower,
Stood on the steps and waited for the hour,
Swaying among the cackling hens and cocks.
And the bells rang and rang. You heard the shocks
Of all the peals ringing along the hills.
And with the wedding-guests the garden fills.
And now they form, and in procession slow
After the pallid bride the maidens go.
A simple music the procession led,
And the poet praised God in his heart, and said:
Thus to the Promised Land of old departed
Rebecca proud and brave and tender-hearted.
Times have not changed if you the Father love.
Perhaps this is the well you bent above,

O Rachel, when you freed your heavy hair
Upon your hands, and Jacob watched you there,
From the palm's shadow, all your hair unrolled,
And your firm cheeks like burnished fruits of gold.

DO NOT CONSOLE ME.

Do not console me.   I should not have heard.
If dreams, which were the only wealth I wist,
Leave my dark threshold whereon squats the mist,
I shall be ready, and shall speak no word.

But some day, very simply (do not cheer me),
I shall stretch myself under the azure sky.
They will tell the children not to come too near me,
And, sadness having left me, I shall die.

GUSTAVE KAHN.
1859-—

I DREAMED OF A CRUEL LAD.

I DREAMED of a cruel lad
torturing a little bird he had,
to feel its flanks palpitate.

I dreamed of a world like a mother's breast
with shades of siesta and slow wings fluttering rest,
and alleys of white dreams.

I dreamed as of a sister, chaste, serene,
with the only lips of sweetness that have been,
sister and wife she seems.

THE PILGRIM FROM THE EAST.

IT is a pilgrim coming from the East.
There had he been to seek a balmy flower
which planted, in the gardens of Engaddi
designed according to the loveliness
of Abishag and of the robes her dower,
Solomon, old Magician with smoked hands
by an eternal prayer to beauty sent.

He journeyed with his staff and cockle-shell,
he slept by sounding waters of cool streams
which under rosy laurels on white pebbles
feign arabesques of silver dragon-flies.
Then, since the mosques from janissaries suffered,
who guarded them with scimitar in hand,
he came in melancholy home again.

He reared his staff against the chimney-stone,
the staff of the long journey,
and watched towards him kindle
the gentle eyes he loved.
And then his staff became a scented stem
flowered with the great white lily he had found not.

Good pilgrim home from the East,
here in thy home is happiness,
and not along the roads with ambush deaf,
And the world is a masquerade,
beside the sweet and delicate face
that by thy hearth-stone smiles.

MY OWN.

My own is beautiful as floated perfume is—
The other day she seemed an opening flower—
My own is beautiful as Angels' flesh in springtime—
The other evening all the sun was on my heart—

Save from my own's lips there is no caress—
The spirit's parks are decked below her lips—
In clamour she is the Temple and in the crowd the
    verge—
The welcoming of my own, the happy season.

The other morning in her sadness was the night of
    winter—
the voice of my own, the faëry of sounds—
For all my life she is an opening flower—
my own is beautiful as resurrection is.

HOMAGE.

Thy arms with bracelets I will deck,
and with a string of pearls thy neck,
and with my lips thy lips.

My fever-floods shall bear thy passion-ships,
and I will bid thy courage flare,
with all my soul on flame,

and I will crown thy hair
with acclamations I will tear
from poets put to shame.

And then thy pardon I will ask
for having done so ill my task
of singing thy perfumèd grace,
and queenly beauty of thy face.

THE THREE GIRLS ON THE SEA-SHORE.

THE three girls on the sea-shore
have seen the Virgin mother passing
along the grave colonnades—
ah ! whence came you Virgin mother

I was sitting at the prow
sailing through the storms of waters
steering towards the colonnade
whence your eyes look on the sea

Ah ! Virgin mother you are alone
your white robe is like a winding-sheet
you have walked on the waters
to come to the colonnade

I have drowned pilot and skipper
I have drowned the ship and the sailors
because upon the storms upon the waters
they would not believe in my mercy

Ah ! Virgin mother our dear smiles
would draw the cord tight round their necks
even to the very cries for mercy
which they would have sent to the sky that is
      starred by your passage unto our colonnades

Ah ! others my merciful maids
have believed who sleep under the waters
I have drowned pilot and skipper
and all alone I shall haunt the short colonnade
my white robe is like a winding-sheet
Ah ! let not your smiles die alone.
leave me all alone under the colonnade.

WHEN THE KING CAME TO HIS TOWER.

WHEN the King came to his tower
the fair one came to him and said—O King

Neither the wives of thy viziers beneath thy gaze like
        opening buds
nor the far-exiled women weeping their barbarian woods
betray the unknown men who turn by turn untie my arms

To suffer far from thee is hard to the soul in flower,
the soul with calling out in vain is languishing ;
this casket of sweets of thine, my body, take it for thyself;
bless with thy hands the forehead I incline

The King made answer from the tower :

This dream of thy coming to reach thy short lips in caress
all the souls of my being were waiting for it in festal dress;
for thy lips and for thy dreams escorted hither in state
spread are the carpets and the lamps are lighted and the
        vows await.
why wouldst thou tarry in lost laughs, where didst thou
        sleep ?

When the King slept upon the tower, the fair sad lady
  shivered.

If thou didst know not it is errantry and truce
love's moment swift that soothes the sting to sleep
I know that it must be unique and as in dream
as towards the shadows paled of death I drift.

YOU MASKS OF THE MASQUERADE.

YOU masks of the masquerade,
pass, you are not she,
for whom my being staggers drunkenly,
pass without me your parade.

You barques to Ophir or to Thule tossing,
pass, you do not carry in your keels
her to whose lips my heart its being seals,
pass without me your crossing.

You songs of festivals from belfries timing
tarry, if the one sung in your chiming
is she who shall be ever loved of me
and cradle me my Destiny.

THE DYING LOVER.

So long as the child preferred to me such and such a
  player of the flute or singer to the zither,
      little I cared
that she loved such and such a player of the flute or
  scratcher of the zither.

By the cross-roads I have fallen struck, struck by the
    thrust of a sword.
Whose? player of flute or scratcher of zither?

How long the night is to be so slow in dying.

JULES LAFORGUE.
1860-1887.

THE SONG OF A LITTLE BOY WITH A HYPERTROPHIED HEART.

My mammy, says the Doctor,
Died because something shocked her,
    Tra-la-la-la !
    My poor mamma.
He says I too shall go
To sleep with her below,
And when my heart beats so,
    It's mammy calling !

When I go out, they all
Say : Why he's going to fall.
    Poor little chappy,
    He's drunk and happy !
For every step I take
I stagger, choke, and ache,
My heart is all a-shake,
    It's mammy calling !

I go out of the town
To see the sun sink down,
    I shouldn't do it,
    But I don't rue it.
The sun's a heart, I say,
Bleeding its blood away !
My heart beats night and day,
    It's mammy calling !

If little Eleanore
Would take my heart before
    It bursts inside me !
    She can't abide me,
For I'm a hopeless case,
And she's a rosy face,
My heart goes such a pace,
    It's mammy calling !

No, they all make me smart,
Except the sunset's heart,
    Tra-la-la-la,
    And my mamma.
O how I wish to go
To sleep with her below !
My heart is beating so,
    Mammy, ain't it you a-calling ?

FOR THE BOOK OF LOVE.

I MAY be dead to-morrow, uncaressed.
  My lips have never touched a woman's, none
  Has given me in a look her soul, not one
Has ever held me swooning at her breast.

I have but suffered, for all nature, trees
    Whipped by the winds, wan flowers, the ashen sky,
    Suffered with all my nerves, minutely, I
Have suffered for my soul's impurities.

And I have spat on love, and, mad with pride,
    Slaughtered my flesh, and life's revenge I brave,
    And, while the whole world else was Instinct's slave,
With bitter laughter Instinct I defied.

In drawing-rooms, the theatre, the church,
    Before cold men, the greatest, most refined,
    And women with eyes jealous, proud, or kind,
Whose tender souls no lust would seem to smirch,

I thought : This is the end for which they work.
    Beasts coupling with the groaning beasts they capture.
    And all this dirt for just three minutes' rapture !
Men, be correct !   And women, purr and smirk !

THE DIRGE OF THE POET'S FETUS.

BLASÉ do I say !   Have done !
Forward, and tear these roots that glue like night,
Through mamma, love of albumen, to the light,
To the rich gracious stamen of the bright
    Rising sun !

— Everyone has his turn, and now I am ripe
To irradiate from Limbos my inedited type !

On ! Break the bar !
Saved from these steppes of mucus, swimming bold
To suck the sun, and, drunk with milk of gold,
Slavering at breasts of clouds through heavens rolled,
And travelling far !

— On the other side, I shall be a soul that dotes
On the freshness blown by the wind through petticoats !

On, on ! and sleep
On the curdled milk of the good clouds that sweep
In God's blue hand, where His eyes in myriads shine,
To be shipwrecked on the land of virile wine !
Now heart be stout,
Now, now, I am getting out . . .

— And I shall communicate, with my forehead towards
the East,
Under species of kisses that know of it not in the least !

Forwards ! Be free !
Shake, knell of nights ! Filter, strong sun of
Heaven,
Farewell, ye aquarium woods, which, hatching me,
Into my chrysalis have put this leaven !
Am I cold ? Then forward ! Ah !
Mamma. . . .

— You, madam, as long as you possibly can do, suckle
This poor little terrible babe that knows such a muckle.

JEAN LAHOR.
1840-1909.

SHUDDERS OF FLOWERS.

In summer eves the flowers have languors of
Women, and suffer as do souls with love ;
Imploring hymens they shall die of soon,
They dream and tremble underneath the moon ;
Yea, flowers have looks like women's great moist eyes,
They are as full of love and coy surprise.
And roses, white as the immaculate globes
That peep from under dark half-opened robes,
Roses amid the darkness green, while sings
The nightingale her moon-imaginings
And dies with passion for their bodies pale,
Roses forth bursting from their odorous veil,
Taken with sudden folly, bow their white
Breasts to the stars that kiss them all the night.

ALWAYS.

All is a lie: love and mind not;
  Dream while desires are sobbing;
Offer to wounds thou canst bind not,
  Thy heart that stays not its throbbing.

Swift burns love to the ember:
  Give all thy heart to thy dreaming,
Desiring, and loving; remember,
  Life is vain and a seeming.

Be proud with a pride beyond taming;
  If sadness thou have, do not show it;
Love, like a king, purples flaming;
  And, being not God, be a poet.

Love life's weariness leavens;
  Naught beside it is real;
Life is the flash in black heavens;
  We see but in dreams the ideal.

Passion alone the abysses
  Lights, while we grope up the rifted
Slopes: our spirit it kisses,
  Ere into the deeps we are drifted.

Let the light that is wrapped in thee flare then:
  Torches are warm from their burning;
Remember the coffin where men
  All must to dust be returning.

The hole still beside us is gaping:
  Ere its dizziness steams up and takes thee,
Let flame be thy spirit's draping,
  And with love, dream, and longing slake thee.

A SPRING MORNING.

THE crimson morning dazzled me mine eyes,
This, and the swarming sun-gold on the sea,
The sea that made me languish with its sighs
As of a woman rolling under me.
And the waves glittered even as tender eyes;
And swarms of white birds uttered joyous cries,

Wheeled, and plunged madly down, their plumes to
    soak
In waves that laughed with long foam as they broke.
The face of all things quivered with a smile;
It was a landscape vast of earth and sky;
And near upon the azure sea an isle,
Still swathed in mist, slept peacefully the while,
A flower in a vase of lapis lazuli.
And, lilies huge upon the heavens piled,
Beyond the cities and the azure plains,
Stretched in the distance giant mountain chains,
Whose summits, on a sky as satin mild,
Mingled their virgin whiteness with the hour's;
And peach-trees pricked the blue with rosy flowers.
Enchanted by the beauty of the scene,
I walked beyond the town, when lo! a child,
Filthy and thin, with holes where eyes had been,
With scanty rags his chilblained body clad,
Stretched out his hand, and raised his face half-mad.
His mother ill, and father he had none,
Never his pain was soothed by a caress,
The sun alone kissed his foul ugliness,
And passers-by were hard to no man's son.
Then I began to muse on Heaven's ways,
On Evil's vulture always eating at
The entrails of the universe, and that
Background of sorrow mute which not betrays
By tears its presence, beings who are bred
By chance, of children for their forbears' sins
Punished, of Life's iniquities, snares, gins,
Horrors and chastisements unmerited.
And near this child with empty orbits, I
Could gaze no more upon the glorious sky
Above earth's blossoming garden, fearing lest
God in His justice meant them for a jest.

PIERRE LIÉVRE.
1882-—.

A GATHERING OF GALLANTS.

WHERE orange lanterns light the gravel walk,
  And rust the leaves of chestnut trees, belated
  Diners in groups familiar congregated
Are mildly entertained by polished talk.

Around blue ponds which falling chestnuts strow,
  Jewels and feathers scintillate and flit;
Sometimes a red point through the night will glow,
    When cigarettes are lit;

And while the smoke of blonde tobacco curves,
  And blends its scent with that of flowers that
      wither,
  You hear a gipsy music wafting hither
Its sweet narcotic to caress the nerves.

WHEEDLING.

WHEN to my powdered breasts I bent his brow,
  How his voice trembled desperately!   Surprise
Melted the hardness of his wicked eyes,
    His heart was yielded now.

Up to my narrow smile his keen lips seethed,
  Under my flowered hat's brim he flushed and paled,
  My corsage, opened half, its scents exhaled,
    Which he with panting breathed.

Then slipping from his hands his rings, while he
  Bared to my kiss his teeth, with firm caress
  And wheedling arms I held him motionless,
    And said : Give them to me.

SENSUALITY.

My fingers squeeze your fat, bent neck, and while
  Your chignon yields and of itself falls down,
  Your capsized eye-balls in your rapture drown,
    Your lips half-open smile.

A hair-pin falls upon your shoulder now,
  And sounds thin on the floor; your arms that beat
  The air with strength exhausted, fondling meet
    With naked wrists my brow.

And in the low room where your mirrow pales
  The many-times repeated round-globed lamp,
  Like a thick vapour in the air's warm damp
    Your perfume floats, and stales.

HEAT.

As tired women languorously undress,
  Summer divests her, breathing roses' scent;
  The mirror in her closèd chamber bent
Palely reflects her easeful idleness.

One single beam through lowered blinds caresses
  And gilds her chignon like a cake baked brown,
  Her fragrant bosom that the sweat runs down
Out of her crumpled linen softly presses.

And while unto her feet her garments fall,
  With brow bent backwards by her unbound tresses
  The summer shuts her eyes, weighs and caresses
One of her breasts with hand mechanical.

PASSION'S BRUTALITY.

SOME Lamia of the night my passion holds,
  Instead of you whose furtive eyes I met
  Flashed through your veil, O you whose silhouette
I gazed on, moulding noble raiment folds.

Your firm-knit figure with its guessed face swims
  Into my longing, and I dream your charms
  Crushed in the hollow of my empty arms,
Your ample bosom and your fleshy limbs.

Your ghost to-morrow from my bed will flee,
  But all one long night-tide you will have been
  The mistress yielded to my passion keen,
Woman whose veiled eyes have not smiled on me,
    And who, perhaps, are chaste.

ORIENTALISM.

SHEHERAZADE, enchantress, love-adept,
  Bring back to me the passion exquisite
  Of queens who, while they pomegranates bit,
Emasculated those who slept with them.

How I desire the wheedling arms of her
  Who would with madness have my love enjoyed,
  I who have only found in pleasures cloyed
Accomplices whom gold alone can stir.

I am sick and tired, at last, of vice's lair,
  Where my sad youth has suffered all distress,
  I know too well the flaunting shamelessness
Of women gathered where shop-windows flare.

Girls from whose pendant breasts the sap is gone,
  They sicken me, and they whose dyed hair falls,
  And they whose red mouth like a sign-board calls,
And those too that you have with corset on.

If sometimes from these joys I have not fled,
  If ever I have sniffed the reek of lust,
  Now from my heart falls down on it disgust,
As an old pillow falls down from a bed.

Stifling I long for distant palaces,
  And for a maid ingenuously young,
  Whose savorous kiss should melt upon my tongue,
Like sorbet drunk from crystal chalices.

She would have thin knees, and her budding breast
  Would hold me till I lost the sting of grief;
  Or she would cool, with waft of handkerchief
'Broidered with two gazelles, my languorous rest.

Her fragrant veils, O cool and delicate laces,
  Would slowly wave.   Her fertile tenderness
  Would every day invent some new caress,
Where fountains play in lonely garden places.

But, a remorseless, shameless despot, I,
  On silken carpets sitting free from care,
  Would follow in my heart a vision fair,
Or ponder, listening to the tales of my
        Sultana with blue hair.

FRANKNESS.

I TELL you true, it is not you I love,
It is not you for whom my spirit pines . . .
If in my eyes my dream arising shines,
As does above a pallid pool the moon,
And seems in rapture exquisite to swoon,
O do not think that such a brief delight
Can be the bloom matured in this one night;
It is not you, it is not you I love,
        I tell you true.

And yet this only night be kind to me.
I am so tired . . . Caress me tenderly,
And let me dream another love than you.
Your care is sweet, my heart is sad and riven.
Fain would it give what unto it is given,
        I tell you true.

STÉPHANE MALLARMÉ.
1842-98.

THE WINDOWS.

TIRED of the fetid smell that climbs and sticks
    In the banal whiteness of the curtains, toward
The empty wall's great sickened crucifix
    The sullen moribund in the sad ward

Lifts his old spine, and, less to see the stones
 Sun-lit than to be warm as can decay,
Glues his white haffets and his thin cheek-bones
 Upon the panes tanned by a loving ray.

His fevered mouth as greedy of azure is
 As when it went to breathe, in days of old,
A virgin skin, and with a bitter kiss,
 Long clinging, soils the lukewarm squares of gold.

Drunken he lives, forgetting strainèd herbs,
 Cough, clock, the holy oils, the bed he dies on;
And when the evening bleeds upon the curbs,
 His eye, where gorged with light is the horizon,

Sees golden galleons on a purple stream
 Perfumed, as fair as swans are swim in trance,
Cradling their lines that with rich lightnings gleam
 In a great sloth steeped in remembrance!

So, taken with disgust at hard-souled men,
 Whose only appetites root in the dung
Of happiness, and, stubborn in the fen,
 Offer it her who suckles them their young,

I flee, and, glued to every window, muse,
 Turning to life my shoulder loathing it,
And in their glass washed by eternal dews,
 Gilt by the chaste morn of the Infinite,

Reflected am an Angel! and I die,
 And love, in panes of Art with mystery gloomed,
To be re-born, dream-crowned, in the earlier sky,
 Where Beauty first burst from its bud and bloomed!

But Here-Below is Lord and King, alas!
   Disgusting me even when I breathe my Rose,
And the vile vomit of the human ass
   Makes me before the azure hold my nose.

Is there a means, I with the Bitter hedged,
   To smash the glass the brute defiles, and flee
Into the azure with my wings unfledged
   —At the risk of falling through Eternity?

HERODIAS.

YES, it is for me, for me I bloom, deserted

Gardens of amethyst, you know it, deep
In cunning chasms dazzled under the steep,
Golds guarding light that once in Eden shone
Under a soil no man has trodden on,
Ye stones whence the pure jewels of mine eyes
Borrow their limpid and melodious dyes,
And metals ye, that in my tresses young
Their fatal splendour and massive lure have hung.
But thou, O woman nurtured in the malice
Of centuries old for caverns sybilline,
Who speakest of a man, saying from the chalice
Of these sky-scented rapturous robes of mine
Should dart the white shudder of my nakedness,
Foretell, that if the summer's blue caress,
For which a woman all her veils unfolds,
My shivering modesty of a star beholds,
I die !

I love my gruesome maidenhood, and will
Live in the terror that my locks distil,
So that, a reptile violated not,
My useless flesh may feel, when nights are hot,
The cold glitter of the pale clearness of thee,
Thou who art dying, burning with chastity,
White night of icicles and cruel snow !

And thy lone sister, sister of mine also,
Who diest not : to thee my dream will mount ;
Truly, so rare is my heart's limpid fount
Already, that I deem myself alone
In my monotonous land where all is grown
Idolatrous of a glass in whose calm sheen
The diamond eyes of Herodias are seen . . .
O ultimate charm, I feel, alone I am.

The Nurse.
O mistress, diest thou ?

Herodias.
                        No, poor grandam.
Be calm, forgive this hard heart, and begone,
But ere thou goest close the shutters on
This seraph azure smiling through the pane,
For I abhor the blue without a stain !

O there are cradled waves, and if thou hast
Heard of a dark land where skies overcast
Look with the hate of Venus burning in
The foliage at eve, there will I go.

Lift once again, though it is childish, I know,
These waxen torches whose fire wan and thin
Weeps strange tears in the flaunting gold, and . . .

The Nurse.

                                   Now?

Herodias.
Farewell.
         My naked lips, your blossom lies.
For radiance never known awaits my brow,
But, ignorant of the mystery and your cries,
You heave the supreme and the bruisèd sighs
Of childhood feeling in its dreamy heart
Its linked and icy jewels snap and part.

CAMILLE MAUCLAIR.

1872-——.

PRESENCES.

I HAVE seen women weave
   Their delicate way through the gloaming,
   I have seen their wraiths go roaming
In the dim and deepening eve.

Their voices in desolate eves
   Died long ago in the doorways,
   Their memories sleep in the porches
Faded along with the leaves.

As a poor man for a bed
   His leaves of gold will heap,
Soul! lay them under thy head,
   Thy memories, and sleep.

And take them unto thy breast,
Warmly under them rest,
So that their perfumes that stain
Thy hands in thy heart may remain.

A MINUTE.

OPEN the door, my daughter, hark !
Someone is knocking in the dark.
— I cannot go to see what stranger knocks,
Before the mirror I do dress my locks.

Open the door, my daughter fair,
There is someone who is fainting there !
— I cannot open now, my hands
Are through my corset threading silk ribands.

O my daughter, open the door !
I am old, I can rise no more . . .
— Father, I cannot go and look,
I am busy with my button-hook.

Perhaps a dead man there is lying,
The wind behind the door is crying !
— Had he been handsome, I had felt the call ::
My breasts have quivered not at all.

STUART MERRILL.
1868-—.

THE ETERNAL DIALOGUE.

THE FLESH.

THE dying sun-god weeps the sated noons.

THE SOUL.

The star of slumber in the heavens swoons.

THE FLESH.

The lilac's languor withers comfortless :
Memory lifts from its grave dead tenderness.

THE SOUL.

The flowers are breathing censer scents : O flight
Up through the blue towards the planet white !

THE FLESH.

Petals of roses shaken in the shower
    Under the winds fly to the vast horizon.
    The kiss of half-closed lips already lies on
Soft budded breasts that burst in dazzling flower.

THE SOUL.

Doves' feathers white and blue are eddying rolled
    Under pale seraphim that pensive pace.
    Among the tombs pray virgins, and enlace
Fine fingers on their missals bound with gold.

THE FLESH.

M'énervent les soupirs, ô Femme que je rêve !
    Et le long des lauriers sous la brise d'avril
Il me faut, au sanglot estival de la sève,
    Tordre ton torse nu sous mon serment viril.

Car le vœu du viol m'envenime les veines,
    Et du fond des massifs les sirènes du mal
Me leurrent de leurs voix vers les voluptés vaines !
    O bouche ! ô croupe ! ô flancs de l'amour animal !

THE SOUL.

The angelus proclaims the dying dusk;
    The valley to the moon steams incense smoke;
    Night folds the plains and mountains in one cloak;
Soul, it is time to strip the body's husk.

From the mountains' mystery to the ocean's ache,
    The wind goes beating the pale gold of eve.
    O dream ! that I could fly to dawns where heave
Oblivion's billows fainting as they break !

THE FLESH.

To die ! Ah not when sap in all the trees is,
    And rises, as the blood is shot to breasts !
    The pipes of desire laugh in the live forests.
Hail ! rosy Eros, King of whistling breezes !

THE SOUL.

Men's mother is not Love, but Death.   Soon sinks
    The sun, and like a wan torch dies : alone,
    Lording the days that are and days far flown,
At the tomb's portals prowling stalks the sphinx.

THE FLESH.

The sky is grey with snow or dark with swallows,
A lover's kiss eternally kiss follows !

THE SOUL.

After the beds of love the winding-sheet,
And kiss of mourning on the waxen feet.

THE FLESH.

I shall be born again, in ruining roses !

THE SOUL.

O death that days and nights and all life closes !

WHEN MARJORAM DIES.

WHEN marjoram dies, in winds that blow,
   And your wheel begins its humming,
   I feel that my dreams are coming
Of the ladies of long ago.

Your fingers fly faster and faster,
   The close-reeled spindles thinning ;
   Sister, what are you spinning,
While you sing of joy and disaster?

Is it shrouds for your love-dreams dead,
   Dead when they saw all the flowers
   That scented the fugitive hours
Die on the garden bed?

When I speak of these your sorrows,
   Your pale hand opens and closes,
   Your hand that blessed the roses
In our love-days without to-morrows.

The leaves of the birch and the lime
   Are on the water falling,
   The autumn wind is bawling,
And the valley is frosted with rime.

Undo—it is time—your tresses
   Fairer than the hemp you spin :
   The shadow on our fingers thin
Our murmured vows now blesses.

Come to me, dreaming as I am
   Of those old castled ladies,
   Come when thy light wheel stayed is,
O my sister of the marjoram.

ROYALTY.

I AM that king of olden times
   Whose city sleeps under the sea,
   With its iron bells that heavily
Through too many springs rang their chimes.

I seem to know the names of queens
   Dead long, long ago in their bowers,
   O my soul ! and faded flowers
Seem to be falling from nights serene.

The vessels that my treasure hold
   Foundered I know not where nor when,
   And I am the madman since then
Who seeks under water his gold.

I long for my olden glory,
  And for all my servile hordes
  To roar my victory towards
The stars, and wave my pennons gory.

With the moon shining into my eyes,
  Calm, and with falchion drawn,
  I wait for the morning to dawn
And trace my sign in the skies.

While in my heart yet warm
  The hope of conquest rages,
  Have I heard, I the victor of ages,
Trumpets that sound through the storm?

Where are the bells that heavily
  Through too many springs rang their chimes?
  I am that King of olden times
Whose city sleeps under the sea.

LOHENGRIN.

WHILE heralds are unfolding, hot with haste,
  The Emperor's banners crimsoning the day,
  The nobles throng in sumptuous array,
And billow round the lists the sun lays waste.

Lone at the river's brim the wan and chaste
  Elsa weeps tears that for the wonder pray,
  But golden trumpets to the welkin bray,
And noisy knights surge round her brazen-faced.

Of a sudden silence, and terror in all eyes,
For, like a dream come forth from seas and skies,
Lo, to the shingles wafted by a gale,

With swan now swimming after soaring flight,
Looms, underneath his helmet's broken light,
The earnest hero of the Holy Grail.

RINGS.

Rings of high heroes casqued for combat, rings
Whose rubies like Hell's blood and brimstone glare,
When, like a Sabbath of lewd witches, blare
The trumpets under standards' open wings!

Rings of old, white-haired men where candles rise,
Red cardinals who the pomp do consecrate
With lifted arms rigid with papal state,
And with the blue disdain in virgins' eyes!

Rings of gold queens in samite black arrayed,
Whose pearlèd fingers star their missals' print,
While moonbeams through the stained-glass oriel
glint,
And in the castle's organ thunders fade!

THE MAIDEN AT THE FOUNTAIN.

Love's daughters bend above the silent source,
Where mystic nenufars that hide their stem
Make hands and lips desire to gather them.

Here, panting, all have halted in their course
Around the water that reflects their eyes
Azured with gazing at the flowers and skies,

Joy holds them rapt.   The maddest of these girls
Holds up her breasts; she scarcely hears her breath
Hiss through the lips her tongue half openeth.

In the lascivious wind her golden curls
Wave from her shoulders to her knees that bend
Above the fountain's marge where eddies end.

Her sisters soon, the brown, the blonde, the red,
Go, fearful of the pool where they are glassed.
Alone, this one remains as though held fast

By the mystery of the source.   Her hands seem
      dead,
Her hands are stirless as a lily's stem,
The light weight of her breasts so wearies them.

The shadow lengthens as the hours sink,
The bell of evening tolls, the violins
Down in the valley tell the dance begins.

She only tarries at the water's brink,
Her gradual voice arises in the rime
Of the loved maiden lost at harvest-time,

Then hushes, grave.   And when, where cattle
      browse,
Cease tinkling bells, in the dusk forest cover,
The wan, mad maiden who desires no lover,

Above her image in the water bows,
And, trembling, where the shady willow drips,
Kisses in silence her unreal lips.

TO EMILE VERHAEREN.

VERHAEREN, name like the loud clash of spears
　Rung to some barbarous monarch in the night,
　Verhaeren, knell that burying the light
Haunts those between whose fingers gush the tears !

Verhaeren, tocsin a doomed city hears
　Through flames, or trumpets deafening hosts in flight,
　Lightning of gold that makes the marshland bright,
O name whose sudden noises fill our ears !

Terror you conjure up, and the death-rattle,
Man with his Destiny in raging battle,
And tongues of fire that to the heavens dart

From burning forests; yet we hear, sometimes,
Like a bell calling from the gloaming's heart,
Love in you dreaming out his tender rimes !

THE WHITE PEACOCK.

THE white peacock in the blue night crying
　Feels that the breeze pale cherry-blossoms spills
Upon his tail; and, dolorously sighing,

The fountains' water that the midnight chills,
　Where in the park the glades with mist are veiled,
Its many-coloured marble basins fills ;

From distant city alleys is exhaled
   To breathe upon our brow this amorous breeze,
With hint of lips uncertain, passion-paled;

And the rich perfume of round orange-trees,
   Which in their jars of terra-cotta deck
And edge the perron's balusters; and these

Whisperings that wind-calm silence comes to check,
   Shiverings of leaves, and dreams of birds, or cries
Of nymphs who feel a Faun's breath on their neck;

Or, as a wordless melody will rise
   Upon her lips who spins the threaded wheel,
A song that to the reeds the forest sighs,—

All tells me now that where white flowers reveal
   The black sward's softness over-starring it,
The Princess with the mad hands soon will steal,

And I shall see her like a phantom flit,
   And sit down at the ancient statue's base
Which figures Love and Hope, and, in a fit

Of passion, like a prostitute, her lace,
   And gold brocade, and broidered jewels tear
From off her raiment, till, with jealous face,

Naked arising in her russet hair,
   She tramples on her trail, and, pale with spite,
Throws all her finery to the peacock there,

To the white peacock in the azure night!

SEVEN PRINCESSES.

AROUND a fountain sitting seven princesses,
  Sadly their hand upon their chin they leant;
And, while they sang of love, into their tresses
  The wavering breeze was blowing jasmine scent.

And one of them would bite the heart of roses,
  Another would the flesh of lilies hold:
They knew where secret sense of things uncloses,
  And in their voices wept fair days of old.

The landscape was a dream: by fountains pearling
  White palaces indented azure skies.
They heard afar off on the shore unfurling
  The ocean, with a sleepy noise of sighs.

Peacocks on marble balustrades were spreading
  Their emerald fans, the sun had climbed noon's steep.
Round was the shadow every tree was shedding.
  They felt their hands were heavy as in sleep.

Around a fountain sitting seven princesses.
  Their sweet names faded long since from my mind.
Were they not Blanche, Laura with auburn tresses,
  Alix, Maleine, Gertrude, and Rosalind?

The seventh, she had no name. She was the nosegay's
  Most radiant flower. And I remember well
She was the goddess of my heart in those days,
  With her great eyes green as a mirabelle.

Upon her face was shadow of black laurels.
  Some dream of grief was in her : you might note
Her breasts of a wise virgin, tipped with corals,
  Lifting with sighs her slender silver throat.

I know not if I kissed her mouth, or followed
  Her steps: she was so wedded to her dole.
And yet the land was like a bed out-hollowed,
  The sky like azure petals that unroll.

Now I forget. O memory of a queen, who
  Was ever in tears, O lost beyond recall
In din of cities, have I ever seen you,
  Sad singer, you who had no name at all?

Am I not verily a poet stricken
  With a dim dream? And, following its flight,
Soothed with an old refrain, while still I sicken,
  Learned from a parchment scroll some outwatched
    night?

Nay, I am certain in my soul's recesses.
  —In a far country sweet with jasmine scent,
Around a fountain sitting seven princesses,
  Sadly their hand upon their chin they leant.

THE FLOWER OF THE HEART.

OTHERS may roses sing,
The flower of the heart is distress.
O ! Life is a dreary thing,
When she you love is merciless.

Love is dead.　She'll tell you why,
Who is laughing in shamelessness.
Poor lover, go thy way, head high,
And never come back in a false dress.

There are other women, they swear,
There is other loveliness.
But this lover loved his fair.
And the flower of the heart is distress.

JEAN MORÉAS.

1856-1910.

THE RUFFIAN.

IN the splendid casket of its scarlet lining
His two and thirty teeth's enamel is shining.
His hair, which once an Abbess loved with sin,
Curled into ringlets in most cunning wise,
Falls—fairylike carbuncles—to his eyes,
Whose curving brows seem dyed with curcumin.

Upon his haunch resting his black-gloved fingers,
With crested cap and trailing sword he lingers
Under high balconies where ladies lean.
His doublet is of silk ; thrust in his sash,
Hilted with silver sheaves his daggers flash,
Set with white diamonds and emeralds green.

And sultry is his alcove with the crushed
Petals of flowers left by great ladies, flushed
With love that cast them panting on his bed.
To kiss his eyes as live as stars, their boons
They bring of jewels, pistols and doubloons,
And bite his lips like slaughtered cattle red.

Thus, handsome as a god, brave as his dagger,
Having killed in a duel the Marquis de Montmagre,
Ten condottieri, four nephews of the Pope,
With calm, high head he marches through the cities,
And drags at his heels women he never pities,
Whose hearts upon his flowering beauty dote.

THE INVESTITURE.

WE will walk by the grating of the park,
When the Great Bear is growing dark,
And, as I wish it, you will wear
Among the ribbons of your hair
The flower called asphodel.

Your eyes in mine will be shining,
When the Great Bear is declining.—
And mine eyes will have the rays
Of the flower called asphodel.

Your eyes into mine will gaze,
And all my being shall with such
A wavering shake as fables tell
The mythic rock felt at the touch
Of the flower called asphodel.

REBUKING JULIET.

To guard you from disaster,
  Love-flags and standards flowing,
I gave you my hair with the sheen of
  The sea when the North Wind is blowing.

Bucklers with mottoes loyal
  Of love and charity,
I gave you my proud eyes to guard you
  From your own vulgarity.

Goblet of music and balm,
  I gave you for your delight,
My live mouth never calm,
  As the rose on the rose-tree bright.

Dames of the wardrobe and chamber,
  To bring you everything,
I gave you my hands that are nobler
  Than the crown on the brow of a king.

And I gave you for your pleasures,
  I gave you heaped on high,
All my spirit's treasures,
  Like pearls cast into a sty.

VOICES RETURNING.

Voices returning, cradle us, cradling voices :
Echoes extenuated of what we love as it passes,
Bells of mules turning the mountain passes,
—Voices returning, cradle us, cradling voices.

Intoxicate us, you also, flasks that prison the yore :
Odours in harvests garnered, fleeces shorn from the hours,
Flesh of amber and musk, mouths of gillyflowers,
—Intoxicate us, you also, flasks that prison the yore.

In this morning of winter, and of shadows chill,
In this morning of winter the voice of the lark is still.
—Voices returning, cradle us, cradling voices.

The lilies are cut in the garden, and every rose,
And the irises by the waters, waters morose.
—Intoxicate us, you also, flasks that prison the yore.

AH WHO SHOULD MAKE MY HEART DESPOND?

AH who should make my heart despond,
My heart untroubled pant and bleed?
Queen Cleopatra it would need,
And Melusina, and the blonde
Aglaura whom the Soldan stark
Sailed away with in his bark.

Since Susan comes a-wooing,
Let us go where the wood-doves are cooing.

My warlike heart no pity has ;
Ah who should make my heart surrender?
Princess Aurelia the tender,
And Queen Ismene whose cheeks surpass
Upon the snows the tints of rose
The morning on the mountain throws.

Since Alice comes a-wooing,
Let us go where the wood-doves are cooing.

ALFRED MORTIER.

1865-——

I ASK YOU, LOVE.

I ASK you, love, to understand but this.
For if you knew how I do love you, naught
Would shock you in my infidelities,
And you would know the reverence of my thought.

These women are not in my heart, be sure.
And you unwisely suffer, thinking I
Prefer a passing drunkenness to your
Reflective fascination, subtle, shy.

What if the body sins? Such luxury harms
The soul no whit. Despise the luring flower
Of carnal lips. Although I love your arms,
It is your soul that holds me in its power.

Your soul, a glass where candid pleasures shine,
Lute touched by mystery's seraph tenderly,
Cup of pure water still refreshing me,
When I am sickened with corrupted wine.

Dismiss the common folly of those wives
Whose mediocre pride makes them enslave
Their husbands in their narrow marriage gyves,
In memory of the maidenhead they gave.

O you my strength and weakness, you I hold
More dear. . .   My love your soul and body mixes
In a miraculous fervour which is bold
To change the postulate that custom fixes.

If I indeed loved but your loveliness,
Then we might tremble for our union . . .
More than unstable passion, we possess
The high, veridical communion.

That of two souls, more than a carnal bond,
For soul alone in hearts ferments, sublime
Folly that builds new beings far beyond
Ignoble luxuries the sport of time.

Now do you understand that my vain rut
Should leave you calm ?   The bonds of flesh are too
Unstable to be crimes.   If I loved but
Your body, I should not be loving you !

MY FRIEND, MY BROTHER.

Not as it seems, friend, brother, is my life,
For I have coveted my neighbour's wife,
His ox, his ass.   And you the woman know
Whom I do covet in my soul's shadow.

Sometimes I wish that God would trouble send
To cross the even tenor of your days.
I curse myself for this, but, brother, friend,
Your generous heart knows not my evil ways.

And you have often succoured my distress,
And warded from my head fate's hardest hits.
But, brother, friend, the heart that ought to bless
Chafes at the burden of your benefits.

Yet if misfortune came, some day or other,
My heart, my vicious heart, content at length,
Would draw, it may be, from its depths the strength
To make your sorrows mine, my friend, my brother.

But you were born under a star that bids
No evil chance or sorrow you betide.
And, friend and brother, always I shall hide
My eyes' cold flashing under drooped eye-lids.

IRREQUIES AMOR.

WHEN for the first time I beheld her eyes
Fixing on me their captions, emerald fires,
I felt Desire, which in our shadow prowls,
Grasping my brain with fingers grimly fierce.
Proud or lascivious, or both, no doubt,
It was a dizzy force that bore me down:
So at the forest's heart the ægipan
Clings to the nymph he meshes in his nets,
Filling the thickets with the cries of their
Two nakednesses panting mouth to mouth.
And then we knew moist faintings, sudden starts
Of strength whipped furious, and Luxury
Distilled the poisons of her flowers upon
The bed in fever from our burning frames.
Insatiable nights curved our hot loins
In the exasperated breath we seethed,
And all the floating sex of greedy lemurs
Curled the shrill laugh uncovering our teeth.

So this was love; this was the mystic rite
Before which stands, like Œdipus before
The Sphinx with tempting eyes, the trembling, grave
Inquisitiveness of our thirty years,
When, cheated by ten years of tentatives,
We dart on love the glance of hasty eyes!
This was the rite . . .   Yet it was beautiful—
For all that flames is fit to serve as torch,
If but the heart, disdaining grief and ruin,
Will raise its torch to pinnacles of stars.
What makes a body dear for evermore?
Haply a soul dwells in the deepest flesh,
A soul more subtle than a thousand laws
Directing choice by rhythms of our veins,
A soul transforming impulse into wisdom.
But, be it what it may, we are the slaves,
Of this malefic and sublime attraction,
Which gladdens even the brows of criminals.

Chimeric thought of prisoning days to be
Within the chains of hope our hands have forged
At twenty we say easily: I love you!
Later, we class love in a system, this
Is still more puerile than young men's love.
Love is all-powerful; love has not the time
To linger o'er our sentimental theses.
We are unconscious Tantaluses, he
Is thirst.
         Shall I some day outlive the sweet
Enchantment and delirium of the flesh,
Which holds already such eternal sense
As never singing chord of lyre can thrill?
It may be.   I dream sometimes of a love,
Of a faith keener than the senses' flame,
And burning in the soul's apse quietly,

As burns a sacred fire lit night and day:
Not Dante's bond with reachless Beatrice,
But living ardour, human and creative,
Yet mystical, an immaterial fruit
Gathered in Orfa's groves by Ariel.

O cup of cheerfulness, O precious pyx
Filled with a wine that but a soul might drink,
O woman holding in thyself this future,
I dare not seek . . . And wilt thou dare to come?

JOHN-ANTOINE NAU.

THE BLUE LAGOON.

TIRED of the flowers' voluptuous whispering,
Nonnoune and Louisy with mixed curls hold
Each other's hand, he pale bronze, she browned gold,
Upon the cliff in happiness bathed deep,
Hearkening the blue chant of the low lagoon.
In this half-foreseen day they have been shown
The force of a word of simple tenderness,
And how a friendly touch grows a caress,
And how much sweeter, once the secret known,
When cheek against belovèd cheek reposes,
And fervid mouth upon the neck's tea-roses.

Under the heavy palms, under the woven tresses
Of the clear filagos—the children with drenched eyes
In irony of pity feel surprise
To hear the turtles weeping in the wood's recesses.

COUNTESS MATHIEU DE NOAILLES.

OFFERING TO PAN.

THIS wooden cup, black as an apple pip,
    Where I with hard insinuating knife
Have carved a vine-leaf curling to its tip
    With node and fold and tendril true to life,

I yield it up to Pan in memory
    Of that day when the shepherd Damis rushed
Upon me, snatched it, and drank after me,
    Laughing when at his impudence I blushed.

Not knowing where the horned god's altar is,
    I leave my offering in the rock's cleft here.
—But now my heart is burning for a kiss
    More deep, and longer clinging, and more near . . .

THE IMAGE.

POOR fawn in a dying trance,
    In thy glazing eye-balls reflect me,
And make my memory dance
    With the wraiths that now expect thee.

Say to the dead that muse
    On the days when they were sprightly,
    I sit and dream of them nightly
In the shadow of the yews.

Praise my forehead wimpled,
   And narrow mouth as well;
Tell them my fingers are dimpled,
   And of grass and privet smell;

That my movements are unencumbered
   As the shadows never at ease,
Which the living leaves unnumbered
   Poise in the apple-trees.

Tell them my eyelids grow heavy
   At times with a pain that hurts,
That I dance at eve with a bevy
   Of maidens with wind-lifted skirts.

Tell them I sleep with my head on
   My naked arms that I fold,
That my veins are a violet thread on
   A cushion of flesh of gold.

Tell them how blue my hair is,
   Like plums that will tumble soon,
That my feet are mirrors for fairies,
   That my eyes have the colours of the moon,

And say that in nights of yearning,
   By fountains as I pace,
For their tender love I am burning,
   And their futile ghosts embrace.

INVOCATION.

PRIAPUS, on thine altar here I lay,
   That thou mayst hear my prayer, thou clement god,
Bunches of parsley and flowered orange spray,
   And, with its green peas swollen, the first pod.

Thou who dost smile on lovers under trees,
  Send me the goatherd Daphnis hard to find:
Eros, begrudging me my spirit's ease,
  Has of his mouth the murderous arch designed.

Why does he not, as others use, with green
  And hyacinth entwine my porch? I frown
On others, and before him none had been
  Who had untied the girdle of my gown.

Thou mightest love me, Daphnis, at the noon,
  And when my goats go grazing, I would sink
Under thy heavy kiss and laugh, and swoon . . .
  And from my beechen cup we then would drink.

See! in my sandals soft and light reclining
  Like two white pigeons are my naked feet;
My slender arms are like to rushes shining,
  As vegetable oils their smell is sweet.

And see my woolly lambs: from their fine fleece
  For our keen kisses we will make a bed;
We will tell by scents when months begin and cease,
  By ripened fruits and roses openèd.

—O syrinx-player! when the red sunset
  Makes the cicada noiseless as his wife,
Hid in the forest teach me, what I yet
  Have learned not, the sweet mysteries of life.

And on the morrow thereof, through the dew,
  To honour better the initial night,
We will go flower-laden, I and you,
  Unto Priapus, god of best delight.

BITTÔ.

THE honey-gilded summer loud with bees,
  Perfumed with lemons, mint, and pine-trees' scent,
Cradles its sensual dream in the sugared breeze,
  And bathes its face in waters somnolent.

The heavy butterflies make languorous
  The flowers, and the beautiful balm-mint's
Rich fragrance mingles with the cytisus,
  While on the smooth trees' bark the sunshine glints.

The elder-branches and the fig-trees are
  Filled with the honey-bees' loud eddyings.
How gay the day and hot fields stretching far !
  The russet meads crackle with noise of wings.

Now here comes little Bittô, sun in eyes,
  Who, when she dances, cymbals beats together;
Her glad feet love the glaring dust that flies,
  And warms them, burning through her sandal leather.

Her veil is of green linen like young grapes;
  Her robe upon her delicate shoulder stirs,
Moving upon the budding breasts it drapes,
  Which are as gay as singing grasshoppers.

Her mirror, scent-boxes, and drinking-cup
  Rattle like pebbles in her basket carried;
She skips along, and sees the bees fly up
  From the rich lips of flowers whereon they tarried.

—Ah Bittô ! what desires your feet impel
  To pathways where the beast in sunshine pants?
Unseen Erotes in the forests dwell,
  And subtle poisons rise from hearts of plants.

Go back and work with other maids together !
   The noon is coming with its shivering light.
Or go into your garden and see whether
   Your green egg-plants have ripened overnight.

But, laughing, from the prudent words she flees,
   Around her supple throat her two hands tying ;
The playful breeze rolls himself round her knees,
   And makes a noise like silken ribbons flying ;

The vegetable balm which round her floats
   With honey light her yielding soul endues ;
She walks through fields of undulating oats,
   And sits down by a pool whose waters muse.

Eager to blend with summer's glorious day,
   The tufted peony and windflower pied
Swoon with desire, and seem to cast away
   Their cowardly corollas opened wide.

What silent, palpitating odours dart
   Around your feet, what god an ambush weaves,
Bittô ? The sun matures and swells your heart ;
   Your heart is trembling like a bush of leaves.

Down the hillside where currants glimmer blue,
   Here Crito brings his goats to the drinking pool,
And in the shade of leaves sees Bittô, who
   Is puffing up her cheeks with water cool.

He hath approached her, saying : " Bittô, take
   This cup that I have carved with tendril shoots
And curling vine-leaves, and this white cheese-cake,
   And this cane-basket where I keep my fruits."

He swears her oaths now timid and now bold,
  He seizes, presses her, he cannot speak . . .
—And Bittô, tired and feeble in his hold,
  Lies in his arms and kisses him his cheek.

 .   .   .   .

After the acrid union O how grave
  And pale she is, confused and full of terror !
—Bittô, you know not what mad impulse drave
  Your heart into irreparable error.

The heavy kiss by poets celebrated
  Brings to the ill you suffer from no ease ;
Your languor came from the green season sated
  With scent of turpentine and mulberry trees.

Thinking to ease your unknown torment, springing
  From all fermenting things the earth that litter
Imprudently your arms you would be flinging
  Round the young goatherd's neck whose kiss is bitter;

Loving the laughing day and light, you thought
  That you could ease upon his lips, that lie,
And speak in frenzy great words full of naught,
  Your desire of air and flowers and waters shy;

O Bittô, it is not for some chance comer
  That with the stress of fever your heart pines !
—The lover that you needed was the summer,
  Sated with scents and aromatic vines !

MY WRITING.

For this I write, that when I lie in earth,
It may be known I loved the air and mirth,
And that my book to future races tell
How I loved life and nature passing well.

Attentive to the toil of towns and fields,
I marked what every changing season yields,
Since water, earth, and flames that gold refine
Are fairest imaged in this soul of mine.

I say what I do feel, what I behold,
With heart for which the truth was not too bold,
I who have had the hardihood to will
When I am dead and gone to be loved still.

And that a young man reading what I write,
Feeling his troubled heart thrilled with delight,
Forgetting those who love him in the life
Should welcome me to be his best-loved wife.

OFFERING.

For you, O youths, the books that I have written,
    In which shall glint,
As in an apple that a child has bitten,
    My teeth's fierce dint.

And I have laid my two hands on their pages,
    And, with head bowed,
Wept as the tempest in the forest rages,
    When bursts the cloud.

And you shall conjure from the bitter prison
    Of this dark book
My drunken soul which, from the dead arisen
    On yours shall look.

My face, a sun to bathe you in its fires,
    To you I leave;
To you my feeble heart that its desires
    Fought to achieve;

My heart of flaxen softness and its story,
 So yielding weak,
And of my hair the blue and ebon glory,
 And the dawn of my cheek.

And see how tattered my poor pilgrim's dress is
 In which your hearts I meet !
The humblest in the wildest wildernesses
 Have not such naked feet.

—And I bequeath you, with its rose-wreathed arbour,
 My garden of July,
Which filled my songs and soothed the grief I
harbour,
 I know not why. . . .

PIERRE QUILLARD.
1864-—.

BLACK FLOWERS.

BESIDE what lakes whose gloomy waters grieve,
 O flowers of darkness vastier than death,
 Do the North's cold gods and Evening's chary of breath
  Your robe of shadow weave?

The sun is swallowed into your deep maw,
 Your widows' veils do make the daylight blear,
 And from the mournful rivers without fear
  Slumber's shy wave you draw.

O dark flowers by the wind of dawn caressed,
 But out of you no scent of love can breathe,
 O dear ones, into hearts that madly seethe
  You pour the balm of rest.

Life spreads perfidious sweets with no avail,
 Spring's purple flames in vain on the young leaf,
 From joy sets free your great redeeming grief;
  Imperious sisters, hail!

Now let me sleep where your dark shadow covers,
 I love you, and your calm I shall not fret,
 And let me far from light and day forget
  The crimson mouth of lovers.

SOLITUDE.

AFTER the winding of the horn
 Through the great silence shivers not a tone,
As in dead towns where cats dream on the worn
 Thresholds of stone.

Under the night's black canopy
 The chargers of the monarchs trampled down,
Through gold and din riding in radiant panoply,
 The blood of roses carpeting the town.

The hours of joy have passed,
And roses on the roadways cast,
And in our tired spirits is forlorn
Silence after the winding of the horn.

THE DEAD GOD.

ONE star shone on the bier, one only star.
　　O solitude where a King's glory died
　　Upon a stake they in the forest hide,
From standards, and the sword, and battles far !

The hero without purple passed, but rolled
　　In faded silk, and in the tresses red
　　Of concubines and captives : lips that bled,
And bit again, and drank the blood run cold,

What kisses did you smile towards?   Towards what
　　　feasts
　　Already ring, O women full of lies,
　　Your chants forgetful !   To make weep your eyes
Were needed some great sack by rutting beasts,

And cold of clarions tearing the black sky,
　　For you to twist your bodies and to grieve,
　　In the red smell of torches in the eve,
Hired mimic mourners under clouds that fly,

But no man's gaze hath from the mounted wall
　　Gathered in greed the flower of your bare arms :
　　You are fled.   The King shall wake at no alarms.
One star, one only star.   O royal pall !

RUINS.

THE illustrious city is a shadowy shape,
　　Turned back into a haunt of grassy peace ;
The broken chapters bleed with ripe wild grape.

And the barbarian shepherd in his fleece,
    Tending his goats among the mallows rank,
Tramples without a pang the soil of Greece.

Neither the oblique sun upon the flank
    Of snowy mountains, nor the dawn upcast
On misty peaks is cause for him to thank

The great gods sleeping in their urns shut fast;
    And when the shagged wild oxen like a wave
Go through the Arch where conquered armies passed,

There is no hero there to draw his glaive,
    But weeds mourn o'er the ruins in the drouth
Of autumn, and in bitter winds that rave.

    Closed with black ivy is the Gorgon's mouth.

PSYCHE.

O MELANCHOLY tender Psyche, sleep.
    Lily of dawn out of the dark hours growing,
    Thy supple arms and lips with freshness glowing
Have made my heart strong with contentment deep.

O little shy white soul, thou hast believed me
    To be what thy virginity desired,
    Nor hath thy kiss of milk and honey tired,
Long as the shadow like my mouth deceived thee.

No word, embrace, nor kisses sick with ache,
    Betrayed the secret, penitential sorrow;
    But wakening with the revealing morrow,
Thy fragile frame would shudder fit to break,

If dawn, which thy serene lids had unsealed,
  Not the sweet conqueror of thy dreamland mists,
  But clenched above thy head, even thine, my fists,
And, rolled in hate and wrath, mine eyes revealed ;

For I hate thee Psyche, with my love's foreseeing,
  For days to come and floods of future tears
  Perfidious, and the lures of wasting years,
Which some day shall gush forth from thy hid being.

But while this night divine is yet my slave
  Let me from metal of sideral deeps
  Fashion the amorous mask a hero keeps,
Laughing as April, and as autumn grave ;

A dead thing that on living lips is laid,
  The mask my writhen face shall wholly hide ;
  And now the first dawn breaks upon a bride,
In whom the woman shall survive the maid.

Awake, and ope thy silent mouth anew,
  From me thou shalt but hear proud words that ring,
  I stand erect beneath my sorrow's sting
Laurelled with gold and like my own statue.

ERNEST RAYNAUD.

1864—.

BRUGES.

O THING of Spain in Flanders left behind,
O idle Delta severed from the sea,
Still worshipping a mystic Calvary,
Singing the self-same tune time out of mind !

The arms of Burgundy and Austria twined
Their glories to be now this ash of thee;
The swan that haunts thy lone canals is he
Upon the proudest blazon e'er designed.

I know thy quays, and nunneries, and the street
Whose grassy cobbles echo to the feet
Of some bedizened soldier of the line.

Thy belfry as thou diest tells the hours,
Shadowing thee like a relic in the shrine
Of thy dead water strewn with willow-flowers.

POETS FORGOTTEN.

POETS forgotten! Unknown poets! Ye
  Beyond the reach of glory! Still I must
Go seeking you along the desolate quay,
  And on old bookshelves mouldering in dust.

And am rewarded when I find some great,
  Beautiful verse full of a rich heart's blood,
  And feel in pride that I am making good,
In spite of gods, the injury of Fate.

O roses faded in the weary years,
  O laurels languishing resigned to die,
How many times, under my lamp, my tears
  Have made you bloom as in the days gone by!

HENRI DE RÉGNIER.
1864-—.

CHRYSILLA.

O GODDESS, when the sands at last are run,
Let me not see slow Time at my bed-head
Cutting without regret or tears the thread
Of an importunate life too long outspun.

Arm rather Love, who from mine hour of birth
Hath hated me, and who were fain to make,
With his last arrow, from the heart he brake
Its pale, thin crimson flow upon the earth.

But no ! Send me my Youth at eventide,
Silent, and naked, lovely as a bride,
And let her shed the petals of a rose

Into the fountain weeping me farewell,
And I shall need no dart nor scythe, but close
Mine eyes, and wander to the asphodel.

THE YELLOW MOON.

Now with a yellow moon this long day ends.
Soft risen in the poplars she with rest
Floods all the air with which the odour blends
From the wet reeds that hide the water's breast.

Did we two know, when over the baked soil
And pointed stubble in a sun that parched,
And on the arid sands we tramped in toil,
With bleeding footprints showing where we marched,

Did we two know, when Love was wild to scorch
Our hearts, and rend them with a hopeless pain,
Did we two know, when in our hearts his torch
Flickered and failed, what sweet ash would remain

At our life's eve, and that this bitter day
Would by a yellow moon be soothed to rest,
Rounded o'er poplars, and by reeds that sway,
And breathe the odours of the water's breast?

THE VISITOR.

THE calm house with the key left in the door,
The table where these fruits sweet to the core
And the clear water-glass show side by side
In the deep ebony; two roads that glide
Towards the horizon shortened by the hills
That dam the sea; so that as clear as rills,
That know not why, my simple laughter rings,
Even as they laugh who never other things
Have sought, except the fountain blue among
High roses, and with grapes their trellis hung,
And in the evening of their life both joy
And melancholy, days that do not cloy
Though each is like to each as glove to glove:
This knew I when thou camest in to me, Love
And didst with woman's mouth bite my ripe fruit,
And drink my water cool from the tree's root,
And, sitting down, didst fold thy wings divine
Over the stones of this fireside of mine.

FOR THE GATE OF THE COURTESANS.

If to the town thou come some morning, to
Join the sweet, frivolous, futile sisters who
Bestow their love and sell their beauty, wait
Before thou enter my returnless gate,
Whose folding-doors are mirrors; there descry
Thy coming self, thou who art tempted by
The gold, it may be, and the banquet's hum,
Thou from a vast and distant country come,
Thou who still pure, and innocently bare,
Smilest, with autumn's russet in thy hair,
And summer's fruits upon thy breast embossed,
And thy soft skin like fabled sea-caves mossed,
And in thy warmest flesh's secret fold
The form of rosy shells the seas have rolled,
And beauty of dawn and shadow, and the scent
Of flowers and gardens, woods and sea-weed blent !
Tarry, ere the ineffable alms thou bring
Of being both the autumn and the spring
To those who far from dawn and harvests live.
Listen, thou mayest yet return, but if
Thou must, I open, glad to see thee pass,
Laughing and double past my double glass.

THE MAN AND THE SIREN.

*Under the last stars of a sea-dawn, standing at the
prow of a vessel unseen, the Watchman speaks. His
voice fades more and more into the distance as the sky
grows light.*

THE WATCHMAN AT THE PROW.

I AM the watchman by the prow . . .
Some sails and anchors know,
Some stars, and others, wiser, throw
The dice, and sleep, whether they lose or gain,
Not caring how
The wind direct the prow ;
But I, I know the Main !

Calm is my Sea to-day under the waning stars,
With a low murmuring creak the spars ;
The sails no more are flapping ;
The wind has fallen, and the tired ship rides ;
Silence is all the sleepers lapping ;
And he who knows the wind and tides
Foretold the night fair while the vessel drifted,
It was with singing that the oars were lifted ;
For he who knows the skies
Hath beckoned laughing to the helmsman at the prow !
Mad is the watcher then, the sleeper wise !
And I alone am listening, watching now,
At-the prow standing while the crew are prone ;
Clear through my dreams I see,
And I alone
I know the sea,
All the sea,
I know that there are Sirens on the Sea !

I know that Sirens sing and comb their sea-weed hair ;
Naked they are ;
The three most fair
Came swimming round the keel ;
They have been seen following the vessel's track,
It was on seas afar . . .

They have not yet come back,
But ever and anon I feel
Their laughing and their singing I shall hear,
When the wave is calm and the sky is clear,
For I, I know the Sea !

And they have sea-weed hair and lips
Dyed with coral's red ;
One sometimes laughs, and lifts
Above the wave her woman's breasts, and head,
And outstretched arms . . .
Some say they are a lure of empty charms,
And that their bodies end in tails,
Blue-seeming under the sea, but clammy scales,
And only in the sunshine seems their hair of gold,
And they are cruel, cold,
And their mysterious laughter lulls to sleep,
For aye,
In rosy grottos deep,
Cheek by cheek with them, men say . . .
And it is wise
To flee them with closed eyes,
And only at the prow
Their simulacrums in enamelled gold,
Cleaving the way to sail !

But I know things within this soul of mine,
For ere I for the oars exchanged the flail,
I swung the scythe, guided the plough,
Eating grapes, and drinking wine,
Which makes the brain see and the dream divine ;
Slept by the naked sickles in the hot corn-lands,
And raised mine axe against the trees,
Where dwell the Dryades :
Their blood has bled in drops upon my hands ;

And saw the Fauns, the thieves of bees ;
And I the Nymph have seen
Laughing from the river at the Satyrs lean,
Dancing with rose-wreathed horn ;
And griffins fleeing from before the Unicorn,
And on the sand with black and reddish croup
The Centaurs gallop one by one and troop by troop !
O memory of my dreams, and all mysterious
Faces which through things look at us, and speak to us,
With voice now high now low,
By you I know
What to believe,
From eve to dawn, from dawn to eve.

Over me
Star by star pales,
The wind blows in the sails,
The wind is crossing the Sea,

There are Sirens on the Sea.

*The blue-tinted dawn grows clearer and clearer. Gradu-
    ally grows visible a shore where a woman lies, naked;
    her head rests on the knees of a youth clad in ample
    and sombre garments. High rocks shut in the view
    behind the narrow strip of shore.*

HE.

This man sings songs surprising,
In the dawn's slow rising ;
Fain had I seen his shadow with the mast
Across the ocean cast,
Perchance I might have spoken with him at his post,
The ship was anchored near the coast ;
But the rocks hid him, and this head,

Heavy and lovely sleeping on my knees,
Has kept me seated with the white dawn on me shed,
And the vessel has lifted anchor in the breeze,
And the Sea is sinking . . .

Heavy is thy head while I am thinking,
O sleeper, that with eyes
Sleepest, thou whose pure and tender body lies
Loose in languor where the sea's
Shells and weeds are strown,
Sleeping in ease,
Smiling and tired and naked,
Soul unknown !

Thy hand the sand caresses . . .
O sleeper when thou awakest,
And standing shakest
Down to thy loins thy heavy tresses,
The soft sand
Will keep the seal of thy rich slumber, and
I shall know nothing of thine unknown soul.

Thy soul is sleeping there while I am thinking,
And I was thinking in the dark,
Long before this voice sang from the barque,
And I was thinking
Of her who came towards him towards her coming,
The stranger woman on the stranger smiling sweet,
And who is sleeping here near him who watching is,
And I of her know only this,
That she is there,
Sleeping at my feet,
Smiling calm and tired and beautiful and bare,
For supernaturally she has smiled, as though
Dreaming, and then I thought she would awake,

But when the slow
Voice of this man sang of the sirens and the sea
She slept again with smiling lips to mine that spake
And heavy head lying upon my knee,
The heavier for her hair of red,
The heavier for her neck outwearièd,
The heavier for her distant thought . . .

Sleeping she ponders things I cannot reach,
I of her thoughts know naught . . .
—Though night is dead, and morning floods the
    beach—
And through her face a face it blurs
Behind her smile seemeth to smile on me,
Other lips allure me behind hers,
And when I gaze into her face I think I see
Someone standing in her and who is my thought
In a black mantle clad.

Her flesh is sweet thus on the sand, her flesh
Is beautiful in this way under the fresh
Pale of this dawn in which my soul is troubled sad,
Because of the soul hiding, alas, within this flesh,
Sweet in its palely living sleep,
Whose closed eyes, and mouth, and belly, and breasts
I touch, whose great gold tresses flow
As sinuous as a sea-weed, and as slow
As a mysterious rolling wave foamed at its crests
Like this pure brow, and sumptuously sweep
To the red sand whereon she lies asleep
A fair enigma, this sleeper I do not know.
For neither her thought is clear,
No, nor the path she wends her, nor her home,
Nor what a fate has brought her here,
At evening when I came upon her near

The ocean marge, pure as she had been born,
Slender out of a shell or white from foam,
Of the shore-sand, or of the salt of the sea.
Is she, perchance, one of the captive girls,
Out of her homeland torn
By some high ship of wood and gold,
Brought to be sold
Upon the mole with birds and coral and pearls?
Wandered her childhood by a placid stream
From willow to willow?
And was her shoulder then an amphora's pillow?
Carried her pious hands the funeral urn?
And did, upon the roadway's asphodel,
Her feet towards a marble palace turn?
Are trees and cities in thy dream,
Or is thy only memory the ocean's swell?
I am thirsty to know thee, O my sister, I will drink
    thy past
As from a spring the willow branches fold
In shadow; rise, O sister, on my shoulder leaning,
And let us walk together, and behold
Our faces opposite each other cast
In the mirror of our double thoughts, whose meaning
Is imaged by our hands together clasped.
Awake, arise!
I can no longer live while thou art sleeping.
I can no longer live till I have grasped
Thy soul, O thou still sleeping
Because thou art to me unknown!
Naked arise, and steep
Thy body in thy sea-weed hair of gold;
Awake out of thy sleep,
If thou so far remainest, O why camest thou
At evening as I paced the shore alone?
It is in thee the sun shall now

Arise, O thou to me unknown,
And thou shalt be !

She stirs in sleep.

The sea ebbs, and this man has ceased his song,
On which thy dream was smiling, as he spake
Of trees whose shade is grave and long,
Of grapes and bees . . .
Awake !
Now he hath ceased
His song of dawn, and crimson is the east !
And let thy flesh still be
Sleeping, but arise,
Out of thyself arise at last, clear are the skies,
And come with me,
Far from the avid sands and the vast Sea.

The sun appears.

*A clearing in the forest. Among the flowers flashes a
deep source of water. High trees around. The hour
is windy and warm ; it has rained ; the leaves are still
dripping.*
*Sitting on moss, websters hold on their knees stuffs
unfolded. They are three speaking turn by turn, the
eldest standing.*

ONE.

Fate of our years and days the weaver is,
Here side by side they sit with us like loves,
While year by year weaves out our destinies.

The wind seems in the trees their wing, and moves
Like Time that fled before us, and is flying ;
The Hours have stolen owls and turtle-doves !

O Life of mine, it seems that thou art crying ;
  The rain-drops are my tears, still comfortless,
O Life of mine, it seems that thou art dying !

I hear thee sobbing in the wind's distress,
  In which the Past, that with my Shadow sleeps,
Sorrows for having drunk forgetfulness

Out of the philtre which enchants and keeps
  The fatal pair locked in my memory's gloom,
Bruising their brow in cracks of ruin heaps ;

And here together they are coming, whom
  My Life draws with her, both in friendly wise
They near me kneel and smile upon the loom

Where I entwine in flowers that them resemble
  Some fabric fate of error and of lies
That makes my hand that weaves it shake and tremble.

ANOTHER.

I through the heavy fabric weave the fleet
  Laces of gold that bind the twisted thread
Of subtle and perfidious deceit.

ANOTHER ONE.

And with the cloth, still naked, I have wed,
  Unravelling its patient, deep designs,
The varying silk where falsehood makes its bed.

SHE WHO SPAKE BEFORE.

Its moire like oily, tranquil water shines,
  And inwardly is quivering, spider-wise,
Spinning a web of intermeshing lines.

SHE WHO SPAKE AFTER.

This silk is soft as human skin, it lies;
  Faces fantastical are fashioned in it;
This silk is vain as is the soul, it lies.

TOGETHER.

Deceitful woman's dress, 'tis we who spin it.

*The choir has withdrawn. The sun is lighting up
the forest again; the water is heard dripping from the
branches; a soft warmth is breathing. Enter the two; he
clad in a dark mantle. She, laughing and languorous,
walking with undulating movement; a light gauze drapes,
like a mist, her naked body. Her loosely gathered
hair half ruins on her neck. Her hand holds roses.*

SHE.

Wilt thou not take
My roses fresh and dewy from the brake?
I knelt upon the warm earth by their stem
To gather them;
Take here the fairest,
I wish thee to respire it, thou who stridest,
And never bending o'er them starest
Upon the ground, yea, I were fain to behold
In these pale hands thou hidest
Under thy drugget mantle's earnest fold
The very fairest of these flowers on fire,
Yea, I desire
That thou shouldst walk before my clear laugh rose in
    hand.

She offers him a flower, which falls when he does not take it.

The rain and sun are weaving silk and gold
Upon thy sombre mantle, brightening thy way;
Light in its woof of joy enlaces thee.
Why art thou sad, and clad
In gloom for ever unbeguiled?
Why hast thou cast my rose away,
And never smiled
To see it sweet and gay!

Dost thou love more
My lips! They still are fresh and dewy, see,
With having kissed the flowers before
I offered them to thee.
O thou who hast but scorn
For roses that I gather from the thorn,
O thou who lovest not the forest smells,
Thou in whose heart, when shines the glad day, wells
A darker melancholy,
As black as in the sunbeams lurks the holly.

All laughs and sings,
The foliage on the flowers and mosses drips,
Wet is the forest far and wide,
Diamonds rain upon the mirror of the springs;
Taste my sweet lips.

Thou pushest me aside.

A cloud passes over the trees,
The sky grows marbled grey,
The forest that was golden is a stagnant green,
Here comes the shower apace . . .

It is going to rain.

The sun shines out again.

I knew that thou wouldst need my lips;
Why are thy hands I kiss so cold
Under thy mantle's fold,
When the smile is going to climb into thy face,
And make thee beautiful and glad,
For all that thou wouldst do
Still to be taciturn and sad,
In spite of this singing wood thou passest through?

Look at the forest raining with sun, and, clear,
Ocellate, rustling and shining tear on tear,
Glaucus with emerald and with gold,
Like a peacock spreading his tail. . . .
See! a drop of water has rolled
Upon my cheek, and trembles at the corner of my lips,
Then slips
Between my breasts, and tickles, cold,
My warm skin till I shiver, somewhat pale;
My hair half ruins down,
And is so heavy with its wet
That its weight wearies me, and weighs
Like gold that melts in a blaze.
O I were fain to sleep in what in me I feel
Of rapture and thy hands upon my neck. . . .

Let thy fingers cross
My naked skin, my skin is moist and sweet;
A scented and a maddening heat
Arises from it, move thy fingers o'er its gloss;
And the odour of all the forest is in my breath. . . .
Spots of my skin are velveted with moss;
To-day it seems that I have flowering breasts;

Were I to weep, ringdoves would echo after,
And bees are scattered through my laughter;
And in the sweetness of the air in which
I stretch my limbs, taller I seem, more rich,
With all the Universal Life of things
Magnificent !
        Hark how the wind, too, laughs and sings,
All the forest rains bright laughter down,
With branch branch intertwines,
And yonder in the distance, through the brown
Oaks, and the green pines,
A graver wind would seem to be the Sea !

Remember, too, the marge of ocean where,
Among the shells and sea-weeds, tranquil, bare,
I slept, and thou didst gaze on me,
Thus sleeping by the quiet Sea !

The wind grows silent, and the source portrays
My visage underneath
Its crown of tresses and of leaves its wreath;
The source is a mirror when no wind is there;
My veil floats round me like a summer haze,
And you would say it was that ancient foam
Proving me risen from the Sea my home;
And I feel with all my warm flesh I am bare,
And the water lures me. . . .
        O how clear ! Toes, knees,
Thighs, and the torrid hollow in the pool !
And O how cool
Must be the body bathing under trees !

I stand at the water's braid,
And my hair is going to tumble down, and mix
With the silver of the water its cascade

Of gold, and my two breasts that fix
Their points aloft, will surge out of my dress
Falling around me, and an instant so
I by the water, where the rushes grow,
And the sword-grass and the iris and the cress,
Shall, like the viewless nymphs that haunt the wood,
Or like the sirens islanding the sea,
Linger before, rose in the limpid flood,
That with its spreading wrinkle circles me,
I feel thee, O thou source of crystal cold,
Rising to my belly from my toes,
And to my breasts and shoulders till, more bold,
Laughing with eyes I close,
I plunge my head,
Leaving between the water-lilies spread
The billowing eddy of my hair of gold.
Dost thou not wish to see me then arise
Out of the water shivering, with dazzled eyes,
And with a laugh in thy embraces sink,
Belted for warm sleep on the reedy brink?

*She has turned towards him. Her half-opened robe shows
her naked. She lifts her hands, holds up her hair,
and stands for a moment against the glowing forest,
which is darkened by a sudden cloud.*

HE.

*Moves towards her with clenched fists, threatening her.
She prostrates herself.*

I will not, no!
O forest laughing vast with gold and sun
To see her naked so from head to toe,
Put out thy waters, roses, trees in flame,

Be dark ! And be thou silent, O thou chaste,
Deep forest, save the one
That covered with black mantle to thee came !
Him who rebelliously now hath faced
Thy kiss immense that stifles him, and grips
And fights it as it rises-to his lips.
O shadowy wind ! Come from thy caves and leaves
Unto this blossoming stranger who makes bare
Her belly while she heaves
Her breasts aloft, and, in her beauty obscene,
Parades her flesh with springtime drunk and summer hair.
Trouble thy water lest she o'er it lean
To look upon it coveting her grace,
And blow thy furious voice into her face,
And whirl beyond my brain in thy wild storm
The words my mouth spoke drunk with having quaffed
    her
Odour of wetted flesh and downy places warm,
Words that the echoes lip for lip have stammered after.
And I, if I have dreamed her by me bare
At ocean's marge in olden dawns, I swear
That I, magician swathed in black
Of science, sadness, and the night's bleak air,
Into her body whence the gods have driven it sought
To summon back
An earnest soul to match my thought !
Why didst thou, woman, come upon my track ?
Now when I sleep I feel upon my hands thy breath,
Breath of thy mouth that save in kisses nothing saith,
Breath of thy laughing lips that lure the bees.
Thy cheek is ever with the sunshine brown,
Thy hair so lightly ruins down,
And when thou dreamest thy breasts palpitate,
And burst forth out of thy transparent gown,
Where thou art lying in the flowers prostrate,

With open eyes, and belly rising as thy pulses beat,
Tired and soft stretching thy animal heat,
Or with thy elbows in the roses—child !
I feel thee odorous and I dream thee wild.
Depart from me, for thou art dissolute,
And I am tired of the gold and amber tufts
That under thy arm-pits curl;
Tired of thy mouth I drink like melting fruit,
Tired of thy tresses that like waves unfurl,
Which I were fain to twist
In my convulsive fist;
Tired of thy breasts thou reachest to my teeth,
Tired of thy belly that beneath
My hand's caress
Starts like a wild beast numb with idleness,
Of all the bestial life with which thy body seethes,
And round thee into the sun-brown summer breathes.

The wind blows.

Go hence, or be another, go, depart,
I am weary of the wallowing beast thou art;
Go hence, ere with my anger swelling like
This wind that growls among the quivering oaks,
Deaf as my wrath and bitter as my hate,
Thy bestial body with this cord I strike,
Until thou bleed under the vengeful strokes,
And flee, with streaming tresses splashed
With ruining leaves, and by the tempest lashed.
And I with tragic, violent hands shall drape
(My hands, alas ! made for the Lamp and Book !)
The mystic fold of my black, heavy cape
Around my hopeless Destiny more grave;
And through the wildering forest I shall look
Upon a mouth crying with desperate pain,

And, rearing with the vast wind in its mane,
The beast with golden hair that licked my hands.

But thou art weeping; and a grave hand now
Seems to be gathering on thy neck the strands
Of all thy hair; and o'er thy tears thy brow
Shows thee a woman almost.   Black the sky,
And now thy flesh is growing pure and shy;
Now in this shadow that is o'er thee cast,
A sacred sister dawns in thee at last:
The sob that has transfigured thee I bless!

The shadow puts her red hair out with ashes;
She is less naked in her humbleness.
Now autumn sprays the wood with russet splashes. . . .
Say, wilt thou follow me to my high house,
Whose silence hears the nibbling of a mouse,
And, with one finger at thy temple, sit
Learnèdly when the shaded lamp is lit,
Exiled and happy in the fireside nook,
Calm idol with thy elbows on the Book
And one hand on its clasp?   If thou wouldst grow
Like to my thought, come to the evening glow,
Following in these thy tears the paths forlorn.
Thou shalt be Woman, in thy tears re-born.

*He points to the websters slowly advancing through the
trees. They are carrying stuffs, and one of them
sandals. They come in a long ray of sunshine
between two storm-clouds.*

Arise, for here the hours are hastening on!
Clothe her with veil and sandals, let her don
The mantle that is clasped, the gown that clings;
Do up her hair in order, let it deck

9

With kindly honey her half-hidden neck;
Silver her collar be, of gold her rings,
For beautiful and noble must be Thought;
Give her the basket now of osier wrought,
And put the door-key in it, and the cate:
Now she is grave and stately and her Fate.
And now, O sister who hast found again
Thy soul amid thy tempest and thy rain
Of tears, O thou whose naked feet have lagged
So long on sands, and mossy ways of ease,
Now let thy step under hard cypress trees
Ring chastely on the path with marble flagged,
And wander till the shade of night has stilled it.

The websters have clothed her with coif and raiment.
They take her by the hand, turning round.

Farewell, O Sea, O Forest !

SHE (following him).

He has willed it.

The wind has grown still, the sun has disappeared; great
*   drops of rain are falling.   The websters remain*
*   alone behind.*

ONE OF THE WEBSTERS.

The forest weeps in shadows growing deeper.
    Sisters, the wind is still, the heavens sink,
And burst in gradual tears as might a weeper.

The iris lifts her urn at the water's brink.
    The fountain is of marble, and of stone
The source, and thorns of brambles rancour drink.

The leaves to-morrow will be shed and strown,
  The rose has been deflowered by the breeze;
The forest and the rain the Nymph bemoan.

For with her mouth smiled Nature; the great trees,
  Knotted and gnarled with centenary force,
Loved her young breasts and hair that swept her knees.

She was the good flesh, pleasure's sweet recourse,
  The cup that life and loving overbrim,
Sun on the flower and sky upon the source.

  The forest she has left to follow him.

THE ELDEST.

Nature was she; Woman was his desire,
  And understanding not why she was bare
He makes a torch from what was made a fire,

From what was dawn and wind and cloud and air
  He makes a tool, a household fire to stir;
But he will curse the day he took her where

Her lamp will set his house on fire, the cur
  Of enmity shall bark them " Woe betide !"
And Death shall o'er his threshold glide with her.

For her dark mantle is with mourning dyed ;
  Cunning creaks in her sandals' prudent pace ;
Her plaited tresses are already pride;

Her veil is lying, her rings' gold is base;
  And like the oaths she swears but to beguile
Is the cold marble of her cruel face.

Sister, I see him weeping for her smile !

ONE.

The white bread that her basket carries is
   The ash of Hope, her nourishment ; and shocks
Of Grief shall ripen on her trellises.

THE OTHER.

The key that tinkles at her belt unlocks
   The shadowy room where lurk with open maws
Unrest that tortures, jealousy that mocks.

TOGETHER.

Voluptuousness that bites and care that gnaws.

THE ELDEST.

Since for the naked Nymph he had no key,
   And clothed her nakedness no dress adorns,
Nor recognized her sleeping by the sea,

Where naked is the Siren, since he scorns
   The Nymph in golden hair, with troubled breath
Let him go seeking problematic morns,

And let the Woman lead him to his death.

*The sky has become pitch-dark.   A flash of lightning
breaks itself like a sword.*

In the setting sun the same strand as at dawn. He is stretched dead on the sand, she is standing near him clad in a sort of glaucus robe, the train of which is twisted like a scaly tail.

SHE.

O my poor brother with thine eyes of dream and
    knowledge,
Thou who didst in the shadows wake,
Sad brother with thine eyes of knowledge and of dream,
Thou who didst in the shadows watch without a smile,
From evening till the slow dawn brake,
Art thou so tired
So tired, my brother, that thou wouldst not live,
So sick of wanting all thy dreams desired,
So sad, my brother, thou at last art lying cold,
Sleeping upon this shore, O thou who sleepest while
The sun is warming me my hair of gold
Alive and rustling and unrolled,
O thou who sleepest!

And yet the flowers scented the lambent morns,
And there were roses in the forest thorns,
And water-lilies in the river shallows,
And all along the ocean's brink
Grew in the rosy sand the faint sea-pink,
And the blue thistles and the mallows.
And I am beautiful and bare and warm,
And sweet to thy lips,
With all my body sweet and with my lips.
And thou couldst kiss my mouth,
And thou couldst touch my breasts,
With both thy hands,
Touch all of me!

Thou shouldst have held my hair, and gathered up its
    strands,
As others yellow sea-weeds do,
Among whose gold are mingled gleams of blue;
Thou shouldst have gazed into my eyes
As into water that in furrows lies
Of sand more soft than cheeks;
Thou shouldst have touched my belly and its creaks,
As with caressing hand one strokes a wave
That swells and with no foam sinks in its swell;
Thou shouldst have followed of my steps the trace,
Singing and living with a smiling face,
And seeking not Fate's foot to spell
On the sand's Book where Ocean every day
Washes the tangled scrawl, thy theme, away;

Thou shouldst have put into my thoughts the brine
Of ocean, passion, and the warm sunshine,
And all my living flesh enlaced with thine,
And my fresh mouth thou shouldst have laid
On thy grave mouth that with its dreaming pales!

I have in me no phantom for thy shadow,
The shadow which thy dream sought I am not;
Why wouldst thou cast upon my flesh the veils
Of heavy raiments and this mantle hot,
Which at my neck chafes with a clasp like nails?
Why with this swathing lie
Hast thou like other women made me, who
Am naked, pure, and living, why
Couldst thou not leave me bare?

O trésses making of the hair
The wind sings through,
And making of the neck a pillow,

For the red gold of your loving billow,
O tresses making of the massed and curved and plaited
    hair
Some evil warrior's golden casque
Where the chimera coils among
Its up-rolled strands to bask
And shoots its tongue
That hisses tapering into ardent curls,
O robes whose train unfurls
Crawling in glaucous, blue, and sinuous scale,
And images on my ambiguous nudity
A fabulous tail !

Painted and fabulous wouldst thou have me be,
Me the simple, me the laughing one,
Daughter of glaucous Ocean and the joyous Sun,
Thus wouldst thou have me be,
I whose fate was to be naked, like
The roses and the sea,
And therefore you are lying dead, O brother,
You with your eyes of knowledge and of dream,
O sweet, funereal lover,
Who would not hear my laugh and loathed
The nakedness you clothed.

O brother, my sad brother lying stark,
Sleep then, sleep into the dark !
Calmly and gravely through
The wood that rustles and the plain that teems
The streams flow to the seas,
And by the source the water-lily dreams,
And there are birds, and roses too,
And bees !
Desire cuts reeds into his mouth to wed
In double flutes, and sings in wonderment that he

Is Life . . .
And thou art dead !

Now here are we, both by the sea.
Thy soul knew not my flesh should be its wife.
It is in vain I have unrolled my hair,
It is in vain I walked before thee bare,
And thou hast passed, and evening opens thee its door, ·
And kneeling life kisses thy lips that speak no more.

She rises.

And here again I stand before the sea.

O sovereign sea
Mounting in waves of foam thy verge,
Rolling along the shore thy convoluted surge,
O sovereign Ocean
Foaming and murmuring in restless motion,
Propitious and maternal to my flesh
Take me, who did depart from thee, afresh,
Take me again undressed,
Cradle my golden hair among thy red sea-weed,
Take my breast's flowers among the flowers thy caverns
        breed,
Swell thy waves against my breast,
Mix with thy shells the onyx of my finger-tips,
And with thy corals my lips,
Make couches for thy echoes of my ears,
Thou sovereign Sea,
O make me one with thee,
Until the day my nakedness again appears
The same emerging from thy surge,
And from my hair thy pearls of foam I comb
To fall upon my breasts one after the other,
When I appear !

O sovereign mother,
Receive me where thy sacred billows break,
I have returned to thee :
Me the Living, me the Naked, take
O sovereign Sea,
Take me again unto thee, naked take
Thy Siren unto thee !

*A higher wave curls over, and carries her away. Then
the sea grows calm, and lies smooth. The gloam blurs
the cliffs and the strand. Gradual stars gem the sky,
and, from very far, at the prow of a vessel unseen, the
voice of the Watchman at the Prow is heard singing:*

THE WATCHMAN AT THE PROW.

I am he who bleedeth at the prow . . .
Some spat at me,
Others have struck my cheek,
And some, more wise,
Drink, and dispute, and for my raiment play at dice,
But I, in nudity,
Am bleeding at the prow,
Am bleeding on the Sea !

Fair is the Sea beyond a doubt
This evening under the stars,
Which, though I do not see them, climb the sky . . .
These purple sails ! Make me a winding-sheet there-
out . . .
I am so weary, let me die . . .
I am tired of my bleeding flesh and of my bleeding
eyes,
And of your cries,
You who have nailed me at the prow,

And stopped my ears with wax, lest I
Should hear the Sirens and not sail them by,
And blinded me,
Lest I the Sirens see,
You who have nailed me here
With laughs that grew
With every nail you drove into
My flesh, you who believed me mad, when I alone
    see clear,
I who saw that Sirens haunt the Sea.
You say that there are none,
You say they do not comb
Their hair of sea-weed one by one,
Smiling above the foam ;
And those who from the soil come, on their heels
Dragging the fat glebe of the cereal lands
With withered forest leaves, upon their hands
Still the heavy gesture of the harrow, axe, or plough,
All those with you deriding,
Crying that I was mad here at the prow,
That in the fields no longer Fauns are hiding,
That in the dark, deep wood
The beeches branch by branch at gloaming fall,
And trunk by trunk, under the hatchet's stroke,
Without the Dryad's blood
Staining the blade withal,
That now no more the Centaur races,
Carrying away the fountain nymph across the plain,
Who naked in the shade laughs on his croup,
And that the time is dead of unknown faces
Speaking into the night or weeping into the rain,
Masks of the cavern where the echoes whoop,
Eyes of the water, faces of the rock,
Fates coming in the night and the tempest's shock,
Signs of the silence and the life within it, ye

Have said that all is dead,
And that our soul has nothing now to see !

Lift
Your oars upon the surge and gold whereon we drift,
Sing in the night and row along the wind,
Not seeing what I see
At the ship's prow where you have pinned
My flesh of a mysterious Argus with your every nail
Like a bleeding, seeing eye upon a peacock's tail,
I, the Peacock of the Sea,
Who proudly tread
And at the prow my bluish wounds do spread.
For I see them,
For I see her,
I hear their voices,
I hear her voice,
There are Sirens on the Sea,
A Siren on the Sea !

ADOLPHE RETTÉ.

1863——

WINTER-SONG.

OUR Lady and her sisters spin the reeling fleece,
   To clothe their bodies who are far from France—
Castle of winter, cloistral peace,
   The joyful flames upon the hearthstone dance.

Spring trills his laughing soul over the snow's soft pillow,
   The gay wheels are whirring round and round :
"Our sweet lords are warring o'er the billow,
   Love shields his minions on heathen ground."

O Ladies, though the brave wheels make a rattle,
   Birds of ill omen on the roofs alight,
   Days are dying, months have taken flight,
Your good lords are dead in battle.

Our Lady all alone spins in the candle-light,
   Her sisters lie beneath the cold gravestone,
Her hair makes her a winding-sheet of white,
   Our Lady falls on sleeping in her bower all alone.

Listen, O listen, lady, now thy spinning finished is :
   The wind is weeping under the porches,
   The wind this night has blown aslant the torches,
Is it not blood staining the panoplies ? . . .

Ah ! the wind moans low like a sick child afraid—
The good knights are dead in the Crusade.

ARTHUR RIMBAUD.

1854-1891.

THE VOWELS.

Ye vowels, A black, E white, I red, U green, O blue,
   I will reveal your latent births one of these days.
   A, of big burnished flies the ebon hairy stays
Buzzing o'er cruel stenches, gulfs of shade ; E, hue

Of tents and vapours, lance of proud glaciers, rajahs
    who
In linen glitter, umbel shiverings; I, displays
Of purples, laugh of lovely lips where angers blaze,
Expectorated blood, excesses steeped in rue.
U, the divine vibration of green seas,
Æons, the peace of cattle-studded leas,
Lines drawn by alchemy on studious foreheads wise.
O, supreme clarion full of strident noises strange,
Silences where worlds and angels range,
O, the Omega, and the violet ray of His eyes!

SLEEP.

A VERDANT hollow where a brook sings loud,
    And madly hangs the grass with silver rags,
Whereon the sun shines, of the mountain proud,
    A little frothing coomb that drunken brags.

A soldier, young, with open mouth, bare head,
    Bathing his nape in fresh blue cress, remains
Stretched out beneath the skies in grassy bed,
    Pale sleeping where the light upon him rains.

His feet are in the rushes. And his smile
Is like a feverish child's. He sleeps awhile.
Cradle him warmly, brook, on thy cold bank.

His nostrils stir not at the scents around.
One hand is on his breast. He sleeps profound.
And there are two red holes in his right flank.

SENSATION.

IN summer evenings blue, pricked by the wheat
  On rustic paths the thin grass I shall tread,
And feel its freshness underneath my feet,
  And, dreaming, let the wind bathe my bare head.

I shall not speak, nor think, but, walking slow
  Through Nature, I shall rove with Love my guide,
As gipsies wander, where, they do not know,
  Happy as one walks by a woman's side.

WAIFS AND STRAYS.

BLACK in the fog and in the snow,
Where the great air-hole windows glow,
    With rounded rumps,

Upon their knees five urchins squat,
Looking down where the baker, hot,
    The thick dough thumps.

They watch his white arm turn the bread,
Ere through an opening flaming red
    The loaf he flings.

They hear the good bread baking, while
The chubby baker with a smile
    An old tune sings.

Breathing the warmth into their soul,
They squat around the red air-hole,
    As a breast warm.

And when, for feasters' midnight bout,
The ready bread is taken out,
    In a cake's form ;

And while beneath the blackened beams,
Sings every crust of golden gleams,
    While the cricket brags,

The hole breathes warmth into the night,
And into them life and delight,
    Under their rags,

And the urchins covered with hoar-frost,
On billows of enchantment tossed
    Their little souls,

Glue to the grate their little rosy
Noses, singing through the cosy
    Glowing holes,

But with low voices like a prayer,
Bending down to the light down there,
    Where heaven gleams.

— So eager that they burst their breeches,
And in the winter wind that screeches
    Their linen streams.

THE SEEKERS OF LICE.

WHEN the child's forehead, full of torments red,
  Implores the swarm of white dreams hovering dim,
Two elder sisters take him from his bed,
  Sisters with silvery nails and fingers slim,

And seat him near a window opened wide,
  Where tangled flowers are flooded with blue air ;
Their terrible and delicate fingers glide,
  Full of enchantment, through his heavy hair.

He hears their timid breath, and, flowering it,
  Long vegetal and rosy honies sing,
But broken by a whistling sometimes, spit
  Sucked on the lip, kiss of imagining.

He hears their black lids beating ; and their mild,
  Electric fingers, in the scented breath
Of silence that in greyness folds the child,
  On royal nails crack little lice to death.

And in him mounts the wine of idlenesses,
  Harmonica that well might rave but sighs ;
And in his heart, in tact with the caresses,
  A ceaseless wish of weeping starts and dies.

PAUL-NAPOLÉON ROINARD.

1856-—.

CONJUGAL EVOCATIONS.

THE honeymoon's last quarter waning thin,
  They judged each other, very haggard he,
  With chin on breast, fresher and fresher she
With irony in the colour of her skin.

Nor pleasure given nor hope for babe can fire
   Her sterile listlessness to fold and flash,
   And the refinements of the husband clash
With his half-weary wish to be a sire.

His long days spent in planning some caress
   Whose keen surprise should set the night ablaze,
   Leave to him vanquished but the cold amaze
Of having wakened only weariness.

Then delicate fear into his conscience bit
   Lest his endured caress bred but disgust,
   And so from chanceful women serving lust
He asked the flesh that for his own was fit.

Weeping her heart unfathomed and exiled,
   Her eyes proclaimed her loneliness, and told
   Her longing for the sister soul you mould
And wed with yours in union undefiled.

Till, tired of questing her appointed mate,
   Her faith returned to the confessor's power,
   And her volubilate voice came back to flower
With serpentine avowals the stern grate.

Then, tired of time by which she was beset,
   One eve her body by the brute *abbé*
   Was seized, and to this traitorous priest gave way,
And by this priest to God, without regret.

Rustic whose frame for labour was too slight,
   Peasant his own despised and made a priest,
   Disdaining the disdain that brands the beast,
He sated his voracious appetite.

She, yielded piously, the Church's prize,
   Love's slave but never conquered yet by love,
   Enjoyed perversely the proud rapture of
Guilty cohabitation with the skies.

JULES ROMAINS.

1885-—.

THE BARRACKS.

Beings have molten forms and lives together.

THE sunshine cannot make the barracks glad.
Its seeming happiness is real pain ;
The building faces to the East ; anigh
Its girdle, forests, fields, and gardens lie ;
Then the horizon furbished by the dawn.

The whitewashed parget walls seem to receive
Only the purest rays that light contains.
The red tiles give the roof a youthful look,
The sanded court is opened like a flower.

And yet the handsome building is in pain.

The clock has just struck eight.   This is the hour
When, in the mighty cities far away,
A rustling of glad bodies fills the morn,
Of men that from the girdle inwards crowd,
Scattered no more by isolating sleep.
A fluid multitude swells streets like veins,
And enters into offices and works.

Shop-windows glass the haste of passers-by;
The omnibuses grate, the chimneys smoke;
Men are connected by chaotic rhythms,
Keen groups are born, and swarm, and are transformed.
Awakened muscles willingly are strong,
Life pours as from a bent, full bottle's neck.

The barracks suffer, wishing back the night.
The soldiers fain would sleep into the dawn,
To be themselves still longer in the dark,
Nestling their liberty in crinkled sheets.

The clarion's panting cries compel the barracks
Once more to don its single, dolorous soul.
Giving to arms no time to stretch themselves,
To hearts no time to glide out of their dreams,
The barracks sets its forces galloping,
And whips at sluggish flanks that hate the lash.
Rest, silence, and the friendship of the dark,
Are with a single impulse thrust outside,
For these impurities would weigh down limbs
Which may not have, until the day is done,
One nerve inactive nor one muscle lax.
The barracks hurries, but the hours are sacks
Too narrow, from too supple leather cut
To hold the heap of movements and of acts
With which it seeks to stuff them, out of breath.

Behind the walls
The vegetating fields lie pensively.
The plants, sure they have time, by slow degrees
Work out their shape, and in themselves unite
The joy of being spreading like a lake,
The joy of growing flowing like a river.
And every time the barracks gazes thither,
It bustles less and feels it is in pain.

Bent soldiers scrub the wooden floors of rooms;
Their backs will have lumbago, arms the cramp.
One was a farm-hand, and remembers now
The music of the scythe in grass of June.
This fair-haired fellow, panting down the stairs,
Is thinking of a little Town-Hall office
With windows o'er a yellow, dozing square;
He used to sit in a cane-bottomed chair,
With glossy paper round his pen, that threw
Upon the left a fibre of blue shadow.
Mud clots the corridors, for yesterday
Was rainy; those who sweep are wearied out;
Others that on the stairheads squat or stand
Are scraping boots while sweat is on their brows.

The traveller who climbs a wooden hill,
And, with his foot upon the highest stone,
Upon it pedestals his lonely frame,
To see the forest and to breathe its breath,
Resumes, for one grave second, in himself
The sap, the sprouting, and the scent of trees;
And if, in all the underwood, one twig
Rises above its clog and sharply cracks;
If strawberries ripen, sheltered by a bush,
One whiff of odour, and one flake of sound
Lost in the smell and rustling of the trees,
Run to the traveller's wide-opened brain
Wherein collected all the forest thinks.

Thus raised more high than any peak of souls,
With effort freed from the entanglement
Wherein its branching passions cross and toss,
And covered with unconsciousness, this dew
Which dropped above the barracks when it passed
The dark, dense flesh that does not know itself,

Already vast but undecided still,
The conscience of the barracks,
From hearts dissimulated among things
Receives the feeble breath their essence scents,
And bids the little griefs sent up by men
Be seated in a corner of its grief,
That they may say in two words what they are,
And what complaints they bear.

This conscience probes the tender epidermis,
Yea, and the final folds of human matter,
Even as a hand that warms and fills a glove.
And, timidly, in places, sees the chiefs
Like scattered seeds of lead within itself.

And then it hears no longer little griefs.
A great wind drowns their wearisome falsetto;
The ardent sex of men begins to cry;
Desire of males in cage calls out for females;
The soldiers sing, roar, jostle, violate
The air.   Their arms seek softer arms to knead.
Furious at having nothing to embrace
Save other stiffened arms that do not yield,
Furious at never finding anywhere
The soft white bodies that are needed for
The barracks to be soothed and have its flesh
In couples equilibrated, they kindle
A fire of frenzied gestures, and their kisses,
Waste cartridges cast in the flame, explode.

And now a locomotive far away
Buries a whistle in the womb of space.
It is rebellion's signal; the clear order
The strength of trains darts unto men's, that they
May break the threads which make them gravitate

Round the same motionless and hated centre,
And from this turning sling escape, and pierce
Their duty like the paper in a hoop,
And the vast soaring rolled in them unfold,
And go away,
And o'er the horizon find their own horizon.

Fain were the barracks to dissolve and die.
There is a breath glides through the soldiers' bodies,
Moving, disjoining, elevating them.
The enormous block seems porous.   All its lives
From one another's hold tear to depart.
It was a serried fleet of sailing-ships;
But the wind whips them and the masts have
     cracked,
The ships are scattered broad-cast on the sea.

O to set out!   The soldiers stamp to go.
Their hope, tiptoe with expectation, tries
To see beforehand the miraculous hour
When all compulsion shall be reaped like hay.
And rude hands weigh the future, feel the months,
And count the days.   And on partitions they
In trembling numbers carve how many more.

By all its men the barracks fain would die.

O this were death delicious as pure water,
If one could be dissolved, and pulverised,
And hurled in ruins by self-hate, without
One atom weeping the dead unity,
And not one being clinging to the warmth
Of living in the rhythm of the whole,
Without the unity bewailing its conscience,
          O beautiful death!

But not in this way shall the barracks die.
First in its leaded coffin it must live.
The State decrees it must exist, endure !
Feeds it with dole of food from day to day,
And fills it yearly with new sap of youth.

Then, one morning, war.

The barracks, that knows nothing,
Shall nothing know.   It will be told
To glide out of its walls,
To march, to follow a road,
To get inside a black train.

And later, not much later,
Not knowing where the carriages
Have taken it to ;
Knowing nothing of all, except
That it must kill ;
Lying flat on its belly,
Leaping like a grasshopper,
Wishing to live now with a frenzied wish,
In mud, and smoke, and din,
Bleeding, raging, thinned,
It will go and will be killed
By canons.

And this presentiment makes weapons shine ;
It spreads a gloss of phosphorus over them ;
The muskets reared in line shine with it so
The soldiers have not for them that kind look
With which you soothe the back of things familiar,
But cast them glances grating on the steel.
The barracks sees that it is filled choke-full
Of muskets, bayonets, and cartridges.

There are erected muskets in the racks,
And in the cellars and the garrets too.
All this swarms germinating in the barracks;
This is the seed!   The barracks knows her sex.
She is prolific.   And she carries, like
A heavy ovary which throbs and swells,
Millions of future deaths within her womb.

The trains may whistle.   What if she forget!
She has her flesh and her fatality.
Fated she is to kill and to be killed.

THE CHURCH.

The self-deceit of having wrought the light.

PEOPLE arrive to worship in their church.

Though it is getting tired and insecure,
The monument can make a gathering yet
With people poured into it by the roads.
It sifts them as they enter through its porch,
And gently it removes from each the thoughts
Which might not melt so well as all the rest,
Replacing them by others left behind
By those who came to Mass in days of old.

The crowd which tramples on the flags outside
Bears nosegays of ideas new and bright;
The fresh dreams of to-day spread over them,
Rosy and blue as sunshades which in their
Own manner dye the radiance of the sky.

Inside there are no nosegays and no sunshades.

The naves and aisles are overflowing with
A crowd the pillars intimately know,
Their contact is as ancient as the church,
And every summer Sunday when the sun
Begins to lick the windows by one edge,
And in the winter of discoloured lamps,
For centuries this crowd has been reborn
On every following Sunday still the same.

Women and men are entering in file.

The crowd is borne in haste by all the doors,
Rumbling an instant, ordered, then appeased;
It has not changed its shape; it is already
Moulded unto the contours of the walls;
Faithfully bodies lean on the same chairs.
Now it is born again while ring the bells.

But the dark power
That gives it life
On the seventh day
Of every week,
Softens at last
Like an old spring,
Little by little
Born less far
From death.

It is a group
Worn out with use
Whose flesh grows flabby.
And in the winter
It is cold
Under the roof.

In olden days,
In the city

It was the greatest of unanimous beings,
And all the city was transfused in it.
But now the workshops have arisen,
The workshops full of youth!
                          They live in ardour.
Their smoke soars higher than the sound of bells.
They do not fear to hide the sun,
For their machines make sunshine.

Like a dog that comes out of a pool and sneezes,
The workshop shivering scatters round it drops
Of energy that wake the town to life.

            But the senile group
            Sprouts not with bristling
            Wires and cables.
            No electricity
            Rustles from it
            To countless houses.

            It is feeble,
            Its chinks are stopped,
            It is gathered in.

But it preserves with pride its fixed idea:
Others may swell with sap and ramify;
And shadow with a foliage of green forces
            . All the massed houses;
The humble group would tenderly, heart to heart,
Speak to the infinite group benevolent words.
For it is sure a soul stands o'er the world.

It knows God's finger painlessly from Heaven
Leads the leash of natural forces;
That God sees all, and that His tender eyes
Wrap up the form and penetrate the essence
Of things.
        The group is sure of it.
                       But fears
Lest having to keep watch o'er all these minds
And bodies, all these angels, beasts, and deaths,
Ant-hills, cities, forests,
Planets and planetary systems,
God see no more the little auditory
Which listens to the Mass in pillared shade.

It calls Him; makes to Him the holy signs.
In olden days God taught His creatures words
Which force Him to give heed and to vouchsafe.

The group that mumbles them knows not their
    meaning,
But knows the priest before the altar knows:
The illuminated summit of the group.

Upon the murmurs serving it as rollers
Slowly the common thought advances, like
A boat that fishers launch into the sea;
        And onward floats the thought to God.

From hearts the fervour passes to the walls,
The rising fluid magnetizes
The steeple, and the steeple brings down God.

        God approaches, God descends;
        He is quite near; the air
        Weighs heavier.

Something compresses, heats it;
The choir is filled with incense
So that, arriving, God
Shall find here clouds
Like those He dwells in,
And feel less strange.

He is quite near, quite near. You can whisper to
    Him,
Tell Him what you would dare tell no man, ask Him
For anything you like. And even if God
Refuse, He is so good you cannot vex Him.

"O God in Heaven, vouchsafe to cure my leg!
Matter burst from it yesterday.—My God,
Vouchsafe to fill my shop with customers!
—Help me to find out if my servant John
Is robbing me!—O God, cure my sore eyes!
—Save me, my God, from getting drunk so often!
—Lord, let my son pass his examination!
He is so shy. Thou shalt have a great big candle.
—Help me to make her fall in love with me,
I will put ninepence in St. Anthony's box.
—My God! if only I could get some work!
—He makes a martyr of me. Let him die!
—My God, my God, I am certain I am pregnant;
O let the child go rotten in my belly."

It is like a hamlet at the hour of noon.
On every soul's hearth they have kindled fire,
Which casts its smoke and yields it to the wind.
God sees the bluish prayers climb up to Him.

They are a perfume which delight Him.　He
Comes nearer.　The crowd rises, touches Him.
Their longing to caress serves them for arm.
They seize on God to press Him close to them;
To be alone and to possess Him all.

This morning, God, the conscience of the universe,
Has from the universe withdrawn, like blood
Out of a bull's limbs bleeding at the head.
All the world's soul, the whole of God is here;
The church is the glad vase that gathers Him.

God now can think but of the little crowd;
The things they wish He too must wish, since He
In them is incarnated and their breath.

> Then in the mystical certitude;
> Drunk with alcohol
> Hid in the organ notes,
> The light of the rose-window,
> And the stained glass;
> Clad with incenselike
> A scented sleep that bends and swoons;
> By old, magnetic ties
> Plunged in hypnotic sleep
> Whence mount, like bubbles
> Crossing stagnant waters,
> Memories and moliness
> And age-old madness;
> Forgetting that bend these walls
> There is the town and earth,
> And then infinity;
> The group so old, little,
> Which withers, which is scarce alive,
> Dreams aloud that is God.

LETTERS.

THESE last few days I have not had one letter ;
No one has thought of writing, in the town.
O ! I was not expecting anything ;
I can exist and think in isolation,
My mind, to blaze and sparkle, does not wait
Till someone throws a blackened sheet to it.

Yet I am short of a familiar pleasure ;
My hands are happy when I break a letter ;
My skin is thrilled to touch the paper where,
Among the folded pages, lingers yet
The immaterial presence of another.

And for three days that I have had no letter
I have been gliding owly into vague
Uneasiness, embarasment of being,
As if I were ashame of my own self.
Intangible remorse sighs on my heart,
Which was not far fm thinking itself good.
My arms are heavy, ix ; I dare not smile :
The air seems to be ngry when I breathe it.
The love around me nd the strength within me,
Disperse. The tow forgetting me, rebukes me.
No one is thinking me anywhere,
No more I am save my wretched frame.
There is an evil tinng in my soul,
An itching in my bn, my fingers' ends,
As if . . . — what ve I done to merit it !—
The city's blood wcebbing out of me.

THE STREET.

I DID not wish to come into this street.

My heart, to be contented, needed now
A boulevard to a Cathedral's base.
Too closely all the houses here embrace;
From window unto window opposite
So short a distance have the smells to leap
I bear them in a tangle on my back,
As though they were the densest fleece of wool.

Too many vehicles run at my left,
Too many shops are masters at my right;
And I am like a wheat-grain pounded by
The stone that turns round and the stone that holds.

So many bodies in some floors vibrate;
So many clerks tread between cubic heaps
And by quadrangular pillars of raw linen
And cloth dyed newly; in the cellar stores,
Near stones and vats there are too many chests
Mewed waiting for a freshening breath of air;
The horses take such trouble not to knock
Their glabrous knee against the wheel of carts;
So many beds, in the darkness, where two bellies
Swell out towards each other like two clouds;
So many movements love, attenuate me;
And, without freeing me from distant places,
Nor even from the weight of other streets,
Without removing from my legs and heels
The viscous mud that after me I drag,
Since through the stagnant soul I lately passed
Of quarters sleeping in the morning sun;

Without preventing the entire town,
With all its houses and with all its trains,
All that is stirring, moving, or at rest,
Being here, more present to me than my heart;
This street, this single street, has so much vigour,
So many ways of reaching, having me,
So many shudderings like writhing snakes
For it to wind and wind about my limbs,
So many rhythms which caress or press,
I have no more the strength to think of it.

ON THE CAUSEY.

A GROUP dies on the causey; I am pleased
As any little lad that pelts with earth.
And now men are dispersing, keeping step;
Suddenly seems one of their steps to kindle;
A jet of gas begins to flame, I love it,
As men love kisses that relax desire.
The rattling of the carriages, I think
That I would linger here for only this,
And budge no more; and this steam-whistle calling,
To hear it, on the causey I would stay,
Having a sweet heart's-shivering at my cheeks;
And for the playing child there I would stay,
Even if the gloaming of the boulevard
Were but this child that sees no more his marbles;
Stay for the maiden who is singing somewhere
Before a candleless piano, while
Her tender body trembles half to feel
The street without crawling against the walls.
Stay for one breath; and nothing is alone,
All holds me.
                    And well I know I must depart.

THE SOUL'S NEED.

I WISH for nothing more
Than my emotion of now ;
There is nothing one is bound to know,
And if my chest inflates,
It is with me it fills.

And yet the breath I exhale
Has the same taste as desire ;
I am not happy yet.

What does my soul need, this eve,
Which is neither itself, nor God ?

.　　.　　,　　.　　.

I should need, perhaps, to tear the alga out,
Roughly, that in bundles ties my limbs,
And which the ebbing tide takes not away.

Then I should feel that I am separated,
And ending in the air, the earth, my skin,
And that my soul no longer feeds poor forces,
And that the blood, here, comes but from my heart.

Then, sure of having myself quite entire,
With the annihilated street curbed under me,
A woman under chestnut-trees would laugh.

And nothing of all that is the world this night;
Nor cattle-herds nor villages of valleys,
Nor yon far army under heaven encamped,
Nor, reading at his lamp, the youth of twenty,
Nor the group eating in the vessel's cabin,
There would be nothing precious more than she.

She would be fain to walk at my left side ;
We should be fain to think our pathways touched ;
And the rhythm would leap from her thigh unto mine,
Imprisoned bird seeking another perch ;
Since I should not have taken her into my arms,
We simply should go walking under the trees.

     -            .   .

I am alone ; but my environs
Suddenly leapt just now ;
They steady themselves ; they palpitate ;
It is as though my hands
Seized and raised from earth
A great swooned body ;
And having puffed my cheeks
I bury my breath in it
Through the slit of its mouth.

A couple passes, groping ;
It is as though my hands
Ferried them down the street.

Another couple yonder
Stop mid in a shadow,
Which docilely begins
To turn around them ;
And from shadow to shadow are kindled
Narrow pointed souls,
Which mount unwavering.
I recognize them from afar,
For they have a dye
Which is that of love ;
And the heat they make
Licks, underneath, the leaves.

TO THE MULTITUDE WHICH IS HERE.

O MULTITUDE !
           Here in the hollow of
The theatre, and docile to its walls,
Thou mouldest to its carcase all thy flesh,
And thy black ranks go from me like an ebb.

Thou art.
           This light that I am in is thine.
Thou hatchest light under too heavy wings,
Loving it, as an eagle loves her eggs.

The town is nigh, thou hearest it no longer,
Although it swell the thunder of its streets,
Even though it strike thy walls and bid thee die,
Thou shalt not hear it, thou shalt be, O Multitude !
Full of thy only silence and my voice.

Warm art thou as the core of flesh.   Thy eyes,
Each of the myriad eyes thou turnest towards me,
I see not if its ball be black or blue ;
And yet I feel it touch me, dart its fire
Into my breast, I feel them all at once
Cross like a million swords beneath my skin.
Thou burnest me.   Yet kill me thou shalt not.

The flame thy bodies can no longer keep
Has rustled along nerves and glances, and
Gathers in me who am become thy crater.

Listen ! The voice is venturing from my flesh ;
It mounts, it trembles, and thou tremblest too.
Test the ascension of my word through thee.

It seeks thee, and it finds thee, seizes thee ;
It circles suddenly thy souls that yield ;
It is in thee invasion, and victory.

The words I say to thee thyself must think !
In ranks they penetrate thy bended heads,
And settle brutally, they are the masters ;
They jostle, push, and thrust outside the soul
That dwelt there like an ancient dame in tears.

All that they pondered on, thy people here,
This sorrow that they drag so many years ;
The grief born yesterday which grows ; the pain
They speak not of, of which they will not speak
Ever, which makes them eat their tears by night
And even this desire which dries their lips,

It must no longer be !   I drive out all !

O multitude !   Thy whole soul stands in me.

A force of steel whose two ends I am holding
Pierces thy body through and bends it back.
Thy form is I.
                    Thy tiers and galleries,
I seize them in my fist and fold them, like
A bundle of lithe reeds upon my knee.

        Do not resist, thou female multitude,
        I is it who desire thee, I will have thee !
        Let all my breath creating thee
        Pass like the wind of the sea.

        The violence of my love
        Has set thy myriad bones a-shiver ;
        This brusque embracing scares thee !

Something in thee would resist,
Thou female multitude, but nothing dares to !

Soon shalt thou die under the weight of thy hours !
Thy men, untied, shall glide out of thy doors,
The nails of the night shall tear thy flesh asunder.
What matters it ?
               I have thee ere thou diest ;
The bodies that are here, the town may take them ;
Keeping a cross of ash upon their brow,
The vestige of the god that thou art now.

ALBERT SAMAIN.

1858-1900.

THE INFANTA.

My soul is an Infanta robed in state,
  Whose exile is reflected evermore
  In mighty mirrors of the days of yore,
In an Escurial left desolate.

And at the foot of her armed throne there gleam
  The eyes of two Scotch greyhounds proud and thin
  That chase symbolic beasts at pleasure in
The forests of enchantment and of dream.

Her favourite page, called Once-upon-a-Time,
  With bated breath reads tales of Fairyland,
  Whilst motionless, a tulip in her hand,
She listens to a mystic, dying chime . . .

The park around her runs its leafy wheel
  With avenues that branch from balustrades ;
  And, grave, she conjures up illustrious shades,
That through the dizzy dusk upon her steal.

Meek is she, unastonished, and resigned,
  Knowing what bitter thing it is to live,
  Dowered with disdain indeed, yet sensitive
To pity as the wave is to the wind.

Meek and resigned even in her sobs is she,
  And only wroth when she evokes some vast
  Armada foundered on the lies that last,
And all great spirits swallowed by the sea.

Too heavy purple eves bow down her pride,
  And Van Dyck portraits in black velvet on
  Old gold of walls, their fingers long and wan,
And their grand airs from empires that have died.

Ancient mirages all her wrongs redress,
  And in the visions that she seeks in dream
  Suddenly—sun or glory—some bright beam
Kindles the rubies of her haughtiness.

But with a sad smile she these fevers stills ;
  Fearing the multitude's loud, iron strife,
  She harks afar, as does the sea, to life,
The while her eyes a deepening secret fills.

No shudder stirs the opal of her eyes
  Where the veiled spirit dwells of Cities dead ;
  She walks through noiseless halls nor turns her head,
And to unspoken words her voice replies.

As might a lorn ship in the harbour wait,
  Pale stands she, with a tulip in her fingers;
  Glassed in the mirrors of old time she lingers,
In an Escurial left desolate.

My soul is an Infanta robed in state.

SUMMER HOURS.

I.

PROLONG our love's contents
  With a pallid wine that gleams
  Through glasses the colour of dreams,
And in exasperated scents.

Roses! O roses still!
  I love them beyond enduring.
  They have the sombre alluring
Of things that we know will kill.

Now summer's gold turns to ashes;
  The juice of the peaches you cull
The snow of your bosom splashes.

Dark is the park, without breath . . .
  And my heart is aching, and full
Of a sweetness that suffereth.

II.

Moon of copper. Air sick with scent . . .
  As under a dome lamps do,
  Stars burn through a balm of blue;
And in velvet flowers somnolent.

The gardens are close as a tent
  That incense sways heavily through.
  And the waters are languorous too
On the porphyries' colours blent.

No leaf's shadow will stir . . .
  Only your red lips burn
In the lifted torch's light;

And you seem, in the air of the night,
  As fatal and hard as the urn
That seals a sepulchre.

III.

Great jasmines opened wide
  The dusk with odours out-wear . . .
  As a bridegroom holds his bare
Utterly fainted bride.

The maddened moth has died
  In the torch's golden glare.
  In the palpitating air
Your eyes dream, opened wide.

Belovèd, your eyes of green,
In the dusk the perfume exhausts,
Are dreaming of tortures dire;

And your nostrils, quivering keen,
In the stifling scents respire
Hearts' bleeding holocausts.

IV.

Flower petals fall.
  Dull flares the torch's mane ;
  Mine eyes to weep were fain,
Mine eyes possess thee all.

Yielded beyond recall,
  Heart, naught shall heal thee again,
  O clay moulded into pain . . .
Flower petals fall.

The roses all are dying . . .
I am saying nothing, thou hearest
Under thy motionless hair.

Love is heavy. My soul is sighing . . .
What wing brushes both of us, dearest,
In the sick and soundless air?

MUSIC ON THE WATERS.

O HARK what the symphony saith,
  Nothing is sweet as a death
  Of music vague on the breath
That a far, dim landscape is sighing;

The heavy night is drunken,
  Our heart that with living is shrunken
  In effortless peace is sunken,
And languorously dying.

Between the cloud and the tide,
  Under the moon let us glide,
  My soul flees the world to hide
In thine eyes where languor is lying.

And I see thine eyeballs swoon,
  When the flute weds the bassoon,
  As though to a ray of the moon
Two ghostly flowers were replying.

O list what the symphony saith,
  Nothing is sweet as the death
  Of lip to lip in the breath
Of music vaguely sighing.

ACCOMPANIMENT.

LIME, and birch, and aspen branches quiver . . .
The moon sheds petals on the river. . . .

Like long hair in the breeze of evening streaming,
In odour lies the river dark and dreaming,
The river like a looking-glass is gleaming.

The oar drips whitely through the dark,
In the dream glides my barque.

My barque glides over the unreal
River into the ideal. . . .

The oars I poise are sister and brother,
One is Languor, Silence the other. .

Row, my heart, by rushes tall,
With cadenced oars that rise and fall,
Row with eyes closed unto all.

The moon to listen leaning on the hill is,
Because the gliding of my boat so still is . . .
Upon my cloak die, freshly cut, three lilies.

Towards thy lips, voluptuous Night and pale,
The pent-up longings of my soul exhale . . .
Hair of the silvered nights combed over reeds that
    quiver. . . .

Like the moon on the reed-beds,
Like the oar on the river,
My soul in sighs its petals sheds.

AUTUMN.

WE in the lonely walk by custom marred
    Pace once again with steps how burdensome,
    And by a bleeding autumn pale and numb
The opening of the avenue is barred.

As in a hospital or prison yard,
    The air is chastened with a sadness dumb,
    And every golden leaf, its hour being come,
Falls slowly like a memory to the sward.

Between us Silence walks. . . . Our hearts do ail,
Each is out-travelled, and its wasted sail
Selfishly dreams of being homeward bound

But on these evening woods such sadness broods,
Under the sleeping sky our heart its moods
Forgets by calling back the past profound,

With a veiled voice, as a dead child's might sound.

EVENTIDE.

INTO the autumn evening's sadness grave
 The panting town exhales its smoke and smut.
 Brother of ease, the river laves the foot
Of ancient towns with legendary wave.

The toilers, that their city labour leave,
 Make ring beneath their heels the bridge's stones,
 Whose soul, with centuries out-wearied, moans
In the indescribable lassitude of eve.

An unseen hand has blessed the cloud ramparts;
 With less of coarseness eye-lids are down-weighted;
 And, like a captive long incarcerated,
The soul an instant in its prison starts.

And in soiled faces great eyes fever-wide,
 And with a plaintive effort poor burnt eyes
 Drink thirstily out of the pensive skies,
And lips are now by silence sanctified.

In heliotrope, with thoughts her fingers hold,
 Revery in loosened girdle passes pale,
 And brushes spirits with her vaporous trail,
To the rhythm of a music known of old.

The West spills roses on the river wave,
  And the wan emotion of the evening dying
  Calls up an evening park where dreameth lying
My youth already as a widow grave. . . .

I see them all, the Beauties of the Past,
  Robed as my credulous heart dreamed long ago,
  Nymphs of the twilight hour they turn round slow,
Upon a distant landscape fading fast.

Caressing, light, as they have ever been,
  I see them with the day's flight blend their hair,
  And, flitting past me one by one, lay bare
My heart upon an ancient mandoline.

I listen . . . and upon the river's brown,
  Below each bridge that frowns like castle-steep,
  Sail slow dream-barks, in which dead ladies sleep
By night on ancient perfumes through the town. . . .

OCTOBER.

TOWARD sweet October pilgrim winter creeps,
  Brushed by the last lone swallow's frightened wings.
  Let us dream . . . the fire is lit, the North wind sings.
Let us dream . . . in ermine ashes the fire sleeps.

Monotonous rain the blackening window sweeps.
  The lamp-shade lights its chastened rose, and brings
  The autumn's chambered sweet rememberings,
Raising the soul foundered in weltering deeps.

The town is far.   Through folded curtains steals
Only the dying din of rumbling wheels . . .
Let us from miniatures frail dreams unlock.

My soul unto a mauve horizon steers
Whose sweetness fades; and from the crazy clock
The hour in ribbons strikes a hundred years.

SLEEPLESS NIGHT.

TO-NIGHT there shall be lighted here no tapers,
    But a sheaf of still wet flowers that shake in frailness
    Shall light thy chamber—where thy tender paleness
Shall like a dream be drowned in white gauze vapours.

That we may breathe a bliss without alloy,
    On the sad piano where the flowers shake
    Play thou a song of angels' hearts that ache,
And I shall swoon into a trancèd joy.

So we will love, mute and austere.   Save this,
That sometimes on thy slender hand a kiss
Shall be the drop that overflows the urn.

Sister !   And in the skies that o'er us bend
The chaste desire of passion taciturn
Shall slowly like a silver star ascend.

YOUR MEMORY.

YOUR memory is like a book we love,
And which our face is ever bent above;
Our heart read into it the nobler seems,
And all our soul is rich with longing dreams.

The impossible I covet: I would dare
Lock into verse the odour of your hair;

Chisel with goldsmith's patient art the word
Trembling upon your lips and yet unheard;
Prison these waves of tenderness that roll
When your dear voice whips tempests in my soul ;
And sing immortally the maddening billows
Tossed in that gulf of breasts that are my pillows;
Say in your eyes what sweets of coolness hide,
Like forest afternoons of autumn-tide ;
Enshrine the relic of our dearest hour ;
And on piano-keys bring back to flower,
Some melancholy eve when memories rise,
The sacred kiss perfuming still your eyes.

MUSIC.

Since there are no words that can hold the brine
   On this sad evening in my soul distilling,
   Let a pure fiddle-bow above it thrilling
Its bitterness of lonely grief refine.

Music! Clear goblet full of memory, thine
   The only water is for the thirst's stilling;
   The soul to be dissolved in thee is willing,
Even as in kisses are desires that pine.

O sob of gold ! . . . O god-like magic ! . . . Fresh
Winds of a wing run o'er the feverous flesh,
And we are by an angel's hand caressed. . . .

Harmony, thou a helpful virgin art,
Cradling like a poor child on thy breast
Our infinite heart, our miserable heart.

ERMIONE.

THE tender sky was strown with roses pale. . . .
   Your eyes dreamed, shadowed by your wideawake
   You floated in your mantle folds; with ache
Of inexpressible things your heart grown frail,

The tender sky was strown with roses pale . . .
Bent over mine like an iris over a lake.

With violets were strown the heavens sad . . .
   And something numb, I know not what, disguised
   Your soul, and your pale smile etherealized;
And underneath your veil your frail face had,

With violets were strown the heavens sad . . .
The softened tones of a Lawrence pastellized.

Yet it was only, in the amethyst
Of evening, souls with meeting glances thrilled,
Sweetness of drops of kisses that distilled,

Yet it was only in the amethyst
Of evening, music of love on senses stilled.

Chaste in the raiment of your soul you walked,
   After you like a tamed wild beast desire.
   And I did in the evening's cool respire
My prowling dream trapped in your veil and baulked.

Chaste in the raiment of your soul you walked,
And in your purity was quenched my fire.

And since I left you, from that hour I keep
  Your mystery with which I am beguiled,
  To translate with the stammering of a child,
The charm of a vague smile on lips that weep,

And an echo of lingering autumn, like a deep
Sob of a horn wandering on waters wild.

ARPEGGIO.

THE soul of a flute is sighing
  At the sounding heart of the park;
We breathe thy silent replying
  Song in the limpid dark,

Night of languor, night of deceiving,
  Who thy dream-hair dost unfurl,
Into it leisurely heaving
  The moon, an Orient pearl.

With your changing blue eyes, ye sisters,
  Clarissa, and Clara, and Kate,
The star in the water glisters,
  Come, ere it be too late,

To the paths where the moonlight is gleaming,
  And gather the sadness of their
Hearts that die of the dreaming
  Of dying among your hair . . .

12

WINTER.

THE sky weeps white tears that freeze
   On the rosy days that are dead;
   And Cupids with chapped skin red,
   And broken pinions, are fled
Shivering under the trees.

The falling evenings have died,
   That we dreamed in the cascade spray.
   Les Angéliques, where are they!
   And their souls, that were ever at play,
And their hearts with ribbons tied? . . .

The wind in the wild-wood rages,
   In the leafage where lovers, wooing,
   Bemoaned their heart's undoing,
   And wove their vows with the cooing
Of the languorous turtles in cages.

The turtles are dead like the leaves,
   The flutes and the violins sigh
   No more, under leaves as they lie,
   Sounds sweeter than words are which die
Along the irresolute eves.

This melody—hark!—the farewell
   Of the last oboe from the core
   Of the forest ere it be frore,
   As if all the days of yore
Drop by drop in the spirit fell.

O glinting satins, O white
   Powdered hair, O muslins fine,
   O Miranda !   O Rosaline !
   Under the stars crystalline,
O dream of the blue ashen night !

O how the brutal wind on the doors as he passes knocks !
The shepherdesses are dead, all, and the shepherds in
   their smocks.

Dead is the gallant folly,
And the Beauty who slept in the holly,
Deep in its age-tangled bowers;
And dead are the sweet-scented flowers !

And thou, O melancholy,
Pale sister of reveries, rise,
Moon of the dead rose skies.

GALSWINTHA.

GALSWINTHA shivering with bowed head does sit.
   Always these unkempt kerns, and heavens dun !
   O her gold land where all the sweet months run . .
And when the dusk comes sobbing into it.

Through her brute husband's halls men see her flit,
   Pallid and frail ; and friends she has not one.
   She kneels for whole days long at orison
In her cold bower by day with candles lit.

Her the barbarian tribesmen almost scorn,
   And slow, and distant in her deep gray eyes,
   She walks with cold tears and with stifled sighs.

And since for such an exile she was born,
How often I with passionate lips have kissed her !
A white corpse in my sweetest heart she lies.

O melancholy vase, Galswintha, my sister !

THE HERMAPHRODITE.

NAKED, the Hermaphrodite is stretched to muse
With writhing reptile limbs upon her bed ;
The jasmine garlanding her short-haired head
And unremitting dreams her green eyes use ;

Her breasts erectile and elastic thews
Excite the neighbouring parts that cannot wed :
A superhuman, exquisite monster bred
In higher skies where forms more subtle fuse.

In her thin, lustreless hair perversity gropes.
Brother of evenings lost down fathomless slopes,
A velvet shadow twists her mouth unsated ;

And her pale flesh she trails with stinging love
Under the pagan sun that bred her of
Thy golden froth, O beauty exasperated !

THE GOLDEN FLEECE.

BLACK in the blue night Argus sails, while dozes
Each chieftain sad, dreaming of Grecian hills ;
Jason alone, who sleeps but when he wills,
Watches, while in his soul his dream uncloses.

The shade is limpid, and the breeze that blows is
  Sweet while the fire-nailed lyre the silence thrills . . .
  Jason with pride immense the horizon fills,
And breathes from far away Colchidian roses.

While he grows drunken with the warm idea,
In the lascivious garden burns Medea,
  And in the breeze from Asia her flesh tingles . . .

The dragon's eye shines as a green pond would,
  And Fate, to brew an ancient frenzy, mingles
With the Golden Fleece the sombre reek of blood.

CLEOPATRA.

I.

LEANING in silence on the tower-rampart,
  The Queen, whose blue hair a silk fillet spans,
  In the troubled incense of perfuming-pans,
Feels, Love immense, thy sea mount in her heart.

On the piled, falling cushions of her seat
  With violet eyelids moving not she rests ;
  The collars of thick gold heaved by her breasts
Betray her silent, languorous fever-heat.

A rose farewell floats on the pyramids,
Eve droops a shadow from his velvet lids ;
  And while afar the crocodiles are weeping,

Clenching her fingers, sighing into the air,
  She shakes to feel lascivious and creeping
  Hands, which in the wind exhaust her hair

II.

The heavy night weighs the dark River down . . ..
　　The Queen, beneath the stars upon one knee,
　　Suddenly pale while all her women flee
With unchaste gesture open rips her gown.

On the high terrace desperately she shows,
　　Love-swollen like a falling fruit, her lithe,
　　Her virgin body that does naked writhe
In the warm and greedy wind, a snake that glows.

She wills, and her wild eyes dart lightnings white,
　　That the scent of her flesh upon the world be
　　　blown . . .
O sombre sea-flower scattered on the night !

　　And the dumb Sphinx feels in his stubborn stone,
Upon the weary sands, a fire awaken;
And the vast desert under him has shaken.

EVENING.

THE seraph of the eve past flower-beds strays . . .
　　The subtle colours of the sunset die
　　An exquisite death, long lingering in the sky ;
The Lady of Reveries the Church organ plays.

Past hearts the seraph of the evening goes . . .
　　The virgins drink love on the zephyr's wing ;
　　And on the flowers and virgins opening
Adorable paleness gradually snows.

The roses bow their heads as night grows darker;
The soul of Schumann wandering through space
A pain incurable seems to be sighing . . .

Somewhere a little baby must be dying . . .
My soul, put in the breviary a marker,
The Angel takes the tears from thy dream's face.

VISIONS.

I.

I DREAMED of a jungle flowered with burning scents,
　Moist with the tufts of musk and creeper glooms,
　Of a jungle of the Indies drunk with blooms,
Where the gold of fertile rottenness ferments.

I was a tiger in the lubric troops
　Of tigresses whose spine was slowly fretted
　With fits . . . while in the grass where poisons sweated
Vibrated love in our electric croups.

The fire of moonless nights our marrows warmed,
And in the dark around us stars that swarmed
Were lit to see us, phosphorescent eyes.

A distant storm prolonged its slow discharge,
And drops of tepid water, like tears large,
Voluptuously fell from great, black skies.

II.

I dreamed an old world with a soul reproved,
　For which My prophet's heart did tender feel.
　My eyes forced Doubt down in the dust to kneel,
And heaven I fashioned when My hand I moved.

Towards My robe came running orphan Pities;
　　And when upon the road I chanced to meet
　　Hope in a beggar's rags, I washed her feet . . .
And incense mildness fell on hills and cities.

Then was I put to death at the Tyrant's hest;
A torrent gushed forth from My bleeding breast,
To be to thirsty souls abundant boon;

To Me were evening hours of prayer devoted;
And in a nimbus of love My pale face floated
At women's sad heart like a mystic moon.

III.

I dreamed a primitive garden, where souls tender
　　In white robes plucked gold clover from its bed;
　　Where azure breaths with warmth were velveted,
And cradled silver flowers like women slender.

On shores of waters shaded by high trees
　　Mystical lovers solitude were dreaming,
　　And ecstasy, and plenary joy were beaming,
And the lambs of God were grazing on the leas.

Love holy, without hate or fever-burn,
Drank at the lips' profound and exquisite urn . . .
O dream-desire perfumed with Heaven's balms!

And I am there among the marjoram,
Virginal, and the bodiless angel am
Whose slender fingers play the candid psalms.

DOVES.

THE weltering sea the bare horizon holds,
The desolate sea where floats the ancient ark,
At whose snapped mast Hope, shivering in the dark,
Her numbed arms on her guileless bosom folds.

For thousands of such years, at fall of night,
The Soul, that steadfast pilot, sees dismayed,
While she is steering through the sobbing shade,
Her doves toward the unknown port in flight.

Scattering their plumes they sweep in search of home,
Through the mad wind that lashes them with foam,
Drunken with soaring where the tempests toss;

And every black and cynic dawn the ark
Sees floating, with their wings spread like a cross,
Upon the ironic sea their corpses stark.

THE EXTREME ORIENT.

AN evening music in the reed was heard.
I went to the river alone. I freed the painter,
I laid me down in the junk was never a quainter,
Noiselessly, not to startle any bird.

And the junk lay on the water like a pillow,
And where it glided knew not. O beyond saying
The charm to be on unknown waters straying ! . . .
And sometimes I bent back the bough of a willow.

And breathed, upon a wave of indolence rocked,
Thy soul, thou evening no sound-shiver shocked,
For subtly I do love the twilight air ;

And sister of my dream sad water that sighs is,
Diaphanous my cup is, and I bear
A melancholy heart where the moon rises.

THE ORIENT.

LIFE is a flower I scarcely breathe, for pain
  Is every earthly perfume after a while.
  My fancy is queen of the Enamelled Isle,
I know men go, and that the hour is vain.

My delicate joys are made of porcelain,
  To keep them whole I use much care and guile ;
  And my yellow tea's blue steam bears many a mile
In scented flight my sorrows from my brain.

I live in a pink kiosk in Wonderland,
And all day long see from my window-frame
The golden rivers in blue landscapes, and,

A royal poet robed in purple dye,
I watch my revery, a butterfly,
Flit round the flowery fan from which it came.

NIGHT OUTWATCHED.

To think. Alone in darkness sybilline
  To shiver ! . . . To be subtle fire around
  The cosmos and refine great thoughts unfound,
And feel one's human forehead grow divine.

To give one's blood the heroic battle sign,
  Not with poor vanity of tinsel crowned,
  But in cuirass of pride with drunken bound
To clear Mortality's dividing line!

To feel sound into one like Ocean's roll
The billow of the universal soul,
To hear that in one's heart all Heaven drifts;

To stand like Solomon, and to behold
One's Work in pomp of jewels clad and gold
Come like the Queen of Sheba bringing gifts.

THE BLACK GOAT.

The Black Goat passes, looking for his bitches.
It is a red, bare night! Thy last shame sinks,
And dies in a pool of enervating stinks;
And midnight sounds at the heart of obscene witches.

Desire's simoon has swept the sweating plain! .
Plunged in thy hair full of an acrid steam,
My flesh hatches thy flesh in a numbed dream,
And breeds the love which turns to hate again.

The lust of each upon the other slakes
Its fury with eyes stigmatized, unsated;
And like to stones our hearts are desiccated.

The Burning Beast has littered on our bodies;
And, as it is prescribed at dead men's wakes,
Our separate souls are praying prone where God is.

XANTHIS.

THE breeze of morning stirs the grasses fine ;
Light vapour floats along the wooded slope,
And, joining tree to tree with delicate rope,
Long iridescent threads unbroken shine.
Close by a brook wrinkled with morning's breeze,
Xanthis, her sandals doffed, robe fallen, now
Leans with one arm against a soft birch-bough,
And, bending o'er the stream, her image sees.
Over one shoulder billows all her hair,
And, white, she smiles to see how whitely lie
Her imaged arms, her narrow waist, her pair
Of rosy-pointed breasts, each polished thigh.
And, with one hand that delicacy guides,
Her young just-shaded innocence she hides.
But a sudden cry makes all the leafage stir,
And Xanthis trembles like a hind at bay,
For she has seen, glassed in the waters gray,
The wicked satyr's horns who loveth her.

ROBERT DE SOUZA.
1865-—.

PLAINS AFTER FAR PLAINS SWEEP.

PLAINS after far plains sweep,
The sky is of velvet above ;
The soul of the limes which is balm
Leads in a soft semi-sleep
The wafting of hours calm,
Warm, and sated with love.

The sky is of velvet above,
The soul of the limes is balm ;
Plains after far plains sweep,
The languorous hours are cradling the calm
    earth to sleep.

ANDRÉ SPIRE.
1868-—.

DUST.

THE SERVANT-GIRL'S SONG.

DUSTER, dust away, my friend,
Never will your dusting end.

I dust it off, and back it falls ;
The chimneys smear it on the walls.

Beat, hands, beat the books,
Whatnots, flower-pots, pegs, and hooks,

Wardrobes, dressing.tables, shelves,
Beds where the kittens coil themselves ;

And, curtains, out of you I shake
The dust your muslin meshes take ;

And, cloaks and petticoats, I beat
The dust you bring in from the street.

Duster, dust away, my friend,
Never will your dusting end.

Take the powder off that lingers
Upon my hair, and rough, red fingers ;

And keep the dust out of my teeth,
Which I can feel it grate beneath ;

And take it, too, out of my ears,
And from my eye-balls that it blears.

But do not let it waft and blow
Into my dreams it dirties so ;

And keep it from the sun-beam spread,
When I awaken, on my bed ;

And from bare statues, and from urns,
Knicknacks, picture-frames, and ferns,

And flowers, and vases ; and we must
Be very careful when we dust

Embroidered robes, and precious laces ;
Rubies and pearls in jewel-cases ;

And gently round the room I tread
Where mistress dozes, ill in bed ;

And now the window panes I clout.
Dust on the highroad blows about . . .

And in the churchyard too, no doubt.

Duster, dust away, my friend,
Never will your dusting end.

IT WAS NOT YOU.

IT was not you I was waiting for,
Always.
It was not you that I saw,
In the dreams of my boyhood's days,
And of my youth.

It is not you I sought
In bodies like a goblet wrought.
It is not you I saw in my dreams
Coming down the hillside, girt with beams.

We were walking on our way.
Our paths met suddenly, one day.
We stretched our hands out to each other.

The days have fled,
My well-beloved.

LONELY.

THEY pity me.
"Look at him, see,
Taking his walking-stick, and going out.   So lonely.
He flees us.   Look at his strange eyes.
Not even a book does he take with him.   Only
His stick.   What does he mean to do?
Is he intent on evil?   In revolt?   Or fever-sick?

Alone, O beautiful white road,
Between your ditches full of grass and flowers,
Over your pebbles telling tales of old,
Alone, O forest, with the blue.bark of your pines ;
And with your wind that parleys with your trees ;
And with your ants processioning that drag
Bodies of little beetles on their backs.

Alone, with you, you sun-drenched fields,
All full of cries, and noises, and heads raised alert,
Alone with you, flies, merlins, buzzards, kites,
Rocks, brambles, sources, crevices,
Fogs, clouds, mists, cones, peaks, precipices,
Heat, odour, order, chaos, and disorder,
Among the dialogues your rival mouths
Exchange for ever !
Alone with my stick, alone with my fatigue,
My dust, my throbbing temples, and my dizziness,
And the proud sweat glued to my skin.

TO MY BOOKS.

You, you have given me my noblest pleasures,
How many times my lips have kissed you, when
I closed you, my dear books.

In you they sleep, frail seeds,
Ready to burst to life again,
The thrills of days departed.

Yes ! more than my parents, much more than my masters,
More than all those I loved,
You taught me how to see the world.

Had it not been for you, I should have lived
Sensible only to the things men do.
Without you, I had been a poor barbarian,
Blind as a little child.

You have dilated all my powers of loving,
Sharpened my sadness, trained my doubt.
By you, I am no more the being of one moment.

And now, now I must take you
Into the secretest room of all the house,
And now with great seals I must seal your door ;
For I will be as though you had not been.

O yes, you books of the past, now I must hide you ;
For I should die cooped at your side.
For you would trouble the eyes you opened wide,
And I should feel you between me and things.

Now I must flee you, like a passioned mother
Who has given her son the suck of all her breast,
And who, in fear that some day he should cease to be
    her double,
Clings to him, crushing him to her violent heart.

Books, set me free ! I am going away to life,
With open arms, bright eyes, and heart all new.
My senses, ardent sons of yours, shall be my only masters.
You shall be outside of me, I will disown you.
Sleep, jealous brothers, in your sombre chamber mewed ;
I go, without regret, without one tear ;
I go made young by my ingratitude,
Vibrating like a virgin, gladsome as a god.

BROKEN BELLS.

O BELLS, you suffer not your gods to die ;
You draw us by our hearts into your churches.

But I see growing the implacable men,
Who do not feel that God must be absolved
Because of your sweet singing.
I hear their dry hymns, and I see their mallets,
And the learned flames that lick their crucibles.

O bells, we cannot do without your swinging.
The bells of oxen they are barbarous still ;
The maidens of our country sing no longer ;
The noises of our forests are too often sinister ;
And when the scythe has mown the murmuring harvest,
Who shall throw joy in human ears,
If you are there no more, bells full of light,
O bells full of the sky ?

You militant voices, flee from positive claws.
As on Good Fridays you were wont of old
To leave your steeples, leave them now again,
But do not go too fast, and look down on our earth.
You will see so many hands stretched up to you
That you will come again to our Town Halls,
To chime the beauty of our new beliefs.

SPRING.

Now hand in hand, you little maidens, walk.
Pass in the shadow of the crumbling wall.
Arch your proud bellies under rosy aprons.
And let your eyes so deeply lucid tell
Your joy at feeling flowing into your heart
Another loving heart that blends with yours ;
You children faint with being hand in hand.

Walk hand in hand, you languorous maidens walk.
The boys are turning round, and drinking in
Your sensual petticoats that beat your heels.
And, while you swing your interlacing hands,
Tell, with your warm mouths yearning each to each,
The first books you have read, and your first kisses.
Walk hand in hand, you maidens, friend with friend.

Walk hand in hand, you lovers loving silence.
Walk to the sun that veils itself with willows.
Trail your uneasy limbs by languorous banks,
The stream is full of dusk, your souls are heavy.
You silent lovers, wander hand in hand.

THE FORSAKEN MAIDEN.

SHE climbed the mountain;
And, naked,
Vaunting her body which he had refused,
She said:
Cloud, stay! O cloud, behold!
And thou, blue gentian flowering at my feet,
You budding larches, bindweeds, you anemones,
You dying snows less lovely than my flesh
Virgin of kisses still, not of desires,
Behold! Behold!
Is not my body worth the love I asked?

Spring breezes mounted from the plain.
Breezes, she said, why will you turn aside?
You pass, I am alone; and I am white:
Winds drunk with pollen, seeds, and hot embraces
Winds bitter with the scent of bodies joined,
Come, take my burning flesh in your moist breathing;
I loved his poor love, more I love your mighty arms . . .
Less my regret is than the bliss you give!

NUDITIES.

The hair is a nudity.

—THE TALMUD.

YOU said to me : But I will be your comrade ;
And visit you, but never chafe your blood ;
And we will pass long evenings in your room ;
Thinking of our brethren they are murdering ;
And through the cruel universe we two
Will seek some country which shall give them rest.
But I shall never see your eye-balls burning,
Nor on your temples purple veins distend,—
I am your equal, I am not your prey.
For see ! my clothes are chaste, and almost poor,
You see not even the bottom of my neck.

But I gave answer : Woman, thou art naked.
Fresh as a cup the hair is on thy neck ;
Thy chignon, falling down, shakes like a breast ;
Thy headbands are as lustful as a herd of goats . . .
Shear thy hair.

Woman, thou art naked.
Thy naked hands rest on our open book ;
Thy hands, the subtle ending of thy body,
Thy hands without a ring will touch mine by-and-bye . . .
Mutilate thy hands.

Woman, thou art naked.
Thy singing voice mounts from thy breast ;
Thy voice, thy breath, the very warmth of thy flesh,
Spreads itself on my body and penetrates my flesh . . .
Woman, tear out thy voice.

FRANCIS VIELÉ-GRIFFIN.

1864-—

NOW THE SWEET EVES ARE WITHERED.

Now the sweet eves are withered like the flowers of
  October
  ⸱⸱What should we tell the willow, and the reeds, and
  the lagoons !—
My soul forever has grown gray and sober ;
—What should we tell the dunes ?

The wind arising comes without a word discreetly :
Fresh with your kisses is my brow ;
The night—as mothers comfort sweetly—
Comes with a cradling kiss to greet me,
What should we tell the willow now ?

While the spring bloomed you were my King, my Poet,
You with your sweet words were the King of Hearts ;
But while we two were laughing, did we know it,
That both of us were playing ancient parts ?

O you and I, did either of us know it ?
—Now all is gray where we would go—
We with our false and honied laughter ?
What knew we of the dark times coming after ?
What did we know ?

There were old poems, doubtless, singing to me;
To you, old tales of fortune crowning doles;
" *You love me then?—I love you!—Love me truly!*"
Were we so young to laugh at our own souls!
What should we go and say now to the dunes?
What to the willow, to the reeds, lagoons?
—The moon is rising in pale aureoles—
Our hearts forgave, and died like misty moons.

HOURS GRAY.

THOSE hours were good to us,
 Like nuns with pity pale.
Sweet hours monotonous,
Drowning in mist, as does
 A sister in her veil.

Those smiles that had not, after,
 The writhen lip of gall,
Were they not worth our laughter?
 Dear, worse hours can befall
 Than those in foggy pall.

They went by sad and swathed,
 As praying nuns do wind,
In gleams of opal bathed,
 The gentle hours resigned.

Our souls are sisters still
 Of hours of autumn gray.
Their gloaming brought no chill,
But blurred our follies, till
 Our hearts were hid away.

ROUNDELAY.

Whether sun or moon is out,
While the wind of May is blowing,
While the trees the grass are strowing,
Lads and lasses dance and shout !
Round and round and round we go
O'er the blossoms' falling snow.
Dark and fair and east and west,
Kiss the one that you love best.

Raise your garlands overhead !
Crimson blood of blazing roses
Blended with the lilies' snows is
Which upon the sward are shed.
And I know the balustrade,
You will lean on, half afraid ;
Look and choose your loveliest,
Kiss the one that you love best.

Laughter, fiddle, flute, and fife
Turn like leaves in the wild wind's eddy ;
Have you got your answer ready,
If he ask you now to wife ?
Take no heed, but laugh aloud,
Speak not, if you are too proud
For your love to be confessed ;
Kiss the one that you love best.

THERE SANG A BIRD.

Behind my father's house there sang a bird,
In the forest, on the lime,
—In olden time—
Across the heavy corn a sunbeam ran,

In the slow days;
A butterfly was flitting through the azure haze
The breeze would fan ;
The future raised fantastic towers above
A river winding far as eye could see ;
They were the castle towers of faithful love.
—The bird sang them to me.

Behind my father's house, there sang a bird
My young dream's song;
And, voice of the plain, and voice of the wave,
And voice of April woods whose burgeons throng,
The echo of the future laughing lied ;
Of the young heart the soul is the mad slave,
And both sang all along
The spring and summertide.

Behind my father's house, on a lime in the wood,
A bird sang of good hope and hardihood,
Life and its joys, tournies, and battlefields,
The lance that shivers and the lance that yields;
The laugh of the lady looking down
Upon the victor from her high turret;
The lady sitting in her silken gown,
And pressing to her heart an amulet.

Behind my father's house, there sang a bird,
From dawn to dusk I heard the song of him;
And in the evenings of my loneliness
His song would haunt me like a long caress;
So long that at the chance of some sweet word,
I called to mind the tunes which I did learn,

Among the mosses and the brakes of fern,
And sang them back again to ladies dim,
Ladies with hair brown, red, or black as coal,
Ladies of mist without a soul.

Behind my father's house, upon the lime,
A bird was singing all the songs of pride;
I stood upon the threshold and I heard ;
The old days of proud massacres have died ;
My prides, that foamed under my will's high rein,
Would rear at any coronation's festive strain,
And they have smelt the flowers of the grave,
Odours of catafalcos bitter and suave ;
My vanities are in their grave.

Behind my father's house, there sang a bird,
Which in my soul and in my heart this evening sings ;
I breathe the burning shadow where a censer swings,
O rutilant gardens where my youth has lain,
And all your seasons, all your hours I live again,
The laughing joy of bright leaves April lies on,
Joy in the blue smiles of the lake on the horizon,
Joy in prostrations of the passive plain,
Joy unclosed in shiverings;
The young delights that filled our eyes
—Rising and setting suns—stars of the skies,
And Life's wide portals open flung
To harvests young !

Behind my father's house, upon the lime,
Behind my father's house, there sang a bird,
In music of flutes and of oboes,
Music that vaunted thee,
Thou, my Dream and my Choice ;
O dost thou know how at the evening chime

My life grew languid listening to the voice;
And from how far my soul has followed thee,
How far thy shadow tempted it to flee
Towards Love's Castle which the bird sang of
In the forest, on the lime?
—In olden time.

BEAUTIFUL HOUR, WE MUST PART.

BEAUTIFUL hour, we must part,
Thou in dream and roses dight
Straying for ever towards the vague and night . . .

And yet I waited for thee like a sweetheart,
I chastened my soul, and made it fit
For thy shoulder's nakedness, whereon alit
My kiss already trembling with awaiting it.

When I lifted mine eyes, far, far away,
Thou it was turning the new-mown hay,
Thou it was in the new vintagings,
And it was thy step, all a shiver of wings.

Thou wert my hope, and now thou art come ere I wist,
Laughing and frail in thy naked beauty, girt
With joy and love, thou who wert . . .
Between yesterday and to-morrow is no to-day,
And thou and I—I swear !—we have not kissed.

DREAM IS CALLING.

STRETCH thyself, Life is tired at thy side
— Let her sleep from dawn till dusk is falling,
Beautiful, tired she lies,
Let her sleep—

But thou, arise : Dream is passing and calling
In the shadows deep,
And if thou shouldst delay
I know not who shall guide thee on thy way
— Dream is passing and calling
Up to the heights of day.

Come,
Take only thy viaticum,
And of all this love which speedeth every step
Take but desire, and go,
But be not slow :
Dream is passing and calling,
Calling once and no more.

Walk in the shadow, run !
Art thou afraid in some abyss to be falling?
Make haste ! . . . it is too late :
Beautiful Life in love-sleep reaches out again
Her gentle arms, thou art embraced
— Too late : Dream is passing and calling,
Calling in vain,
Passing with disdain . . .

Then,
Though Life be tired, kiss her till she surrender,
Of her an art engender ;
If thou didst wend not to God's infinite ways,
According to the Dream which speaketh not but
      prays,
Return, and beautiful Life embrace :
From thy death-pain and her deep joy and good
Breed some melodious song,
Which shall outlast thyself, and, ringing strong,

Laugh and weep when in the joyous wood
Spring roves along
With Love's young ever-to-be-spoken guile.

And sing thou in the radiance of his smile.

IN MEMORIAM—STÉPHANE MALLARMÉ.

IF one should say to you : Master, all hail !
The day dawns on the earth ;
Here is the dawn as ever pale ;
Master, your window I ope,
The morn is climbing up the eastern slope,
The day is at its birth !
— I think I should hear you say : I dream.

If one should say to you : Master, we are here,
Strong, heart and head,
As yesternight we stood before your door ;
We have come laughing, here we stand,
Waiting for your smile and the firm grip of your hand
— They would answer us : The Master is dead.

Flowers from my terrace-bed,
Flowers as in a volume's page,
Flowers, why?
Here is a little of us, songs with our heart's blood red,
Eddying shed,
Even as these leaves fall down and eddying lie—
And here is the shame and the rage
Of living to speak words—when you are dead.

CHARLES VILDRAC.

1882-—.

CHRYSANTHEMUMS.

At the black foot of trellises, by almond-branches
    shaded,
At the heart of corbeils, at the breast of bowers,
And all along the loam of avenues,
Are fallen faded,
Of all smells, and of all hues,
Flowers and flowers.

Lascivious flowers, they all have died
Of loving without rest,
With the sun in rut upon their breast
That odours lubrified.

They have fallen, they have fallen dead
On earth's hard bed,
All the summertide,
Ripe with luxury, with kisses dried,
The bitter flesh of pinks, the irises' black sex,
And even lilies,
Above all lilies.

And from this dung that water fertilises,
From this decay that shadow decks,
Where pallid sunbeams scarce can come,
Marked with anathema arises
The pitiful chrysanthemum !

The pitiful chrysanthemum that blooms alone :
Her gray foot from putrition takes
Her nourishment, and from the bitter corpse of perfumes
    makes
That stinging, vicious odour of her own.

.   .   .   .   .   "

Now, while the arbours in the garden shook,
The sensual virgin tore and took
Chrysanthemums that like the woods were weeping,
And, in their petals her thin fingers steeping
Her vice and fever crushed and kneaded them ;
Her opal, onyx nails took every stem,
And split it, and the drownèd hearts she bruised ;
Then she washed off her hands their blood that oozed,
And, while her young breasts swung, she held beneath
Her nostrils her wet fingers, clenched her teeth,
And fed her acrid instinct with this rot
Arisen from dead autumn's prurient heat.
And, in love's rhythm that relenteth not,
Her nostrils beat and beat. . . .

SONG.

HOPING for nothing, to walk through the streets,
This is a better fate than men believe,
Because you can behold the passing by
Of all the pretty girls there are. . . .

Hoping for nothing, to sail life,
Is all the same well worth the while,
Because of sunny moments, which
It is indeed delight to feel pass by.

Would you perceive that you are very happy,
If you were happy longer than an hour?
Is it not better to have but the power
Of loving with your eyes,
But one poor moment nape, and eyes,
And the mystery that flees with pretty feet
Of all the pretty girls there are?

Come, life is willing to be borne!
Earth is not yet so cold and worn,
And the rare minutes are not yet so rare
In which you tell yourself that life is fair,
In which, quite simply, you begin to live,
In the cool grass, in the warm sand,
Or when your whole mind to the joy you give
Of gathering with eyes the passing by
Of all the pretty girls there are. . . .

COMMENTARY.

Here, before me, the lamp, the paper;
And behind me this troubled day
Passed in myself
Following the hundred turns and twistings of my
    thoughts.

Trying to justify our steps,
And then my steps,
Trying to find my starting-place
Upon my route's confusing plan. . . .

And now, before this paper,
And now, in this my house,
I am still in myself,
And stifling there.

O the great resonant rôles
That all this day I have repeated,
And which, because I can no more improve them,
Now I am going to set down
In my most learnèd eloquence !

Ah my first rôles, costumed in pride,
Moulded in love and bravery,
How they are wearied and humiliated
In this my "theatre in my arm-chair ;"
How they would like to go out just a little into
　　the street !

O all of you whom I resemble,
Have you no pity on us ?
What pure poets we are :
In the warm museum of our chamber,
Our navel marks the centre,
And we examine our own ashes
Behind our bolts.

What pure poets we are,
O we collectors of our fevers,
Who "bring out" our copies of them,
And run, on winter evenings,
To listen to what people say of us !

What pure poets, what pure poets . . .
There are mad oceans far away,
And mad skies, and mad sails,
There are mad vessels far away :
We talk of these in the fine weather,
Leaning at our window.

O you, what men are we?
We are attired in black,
We go to our work,
And when the weather is not very certain,
We take our umbrella.

I am tired of interior movements !
I am tired of interior departures !
And of heroism with the strokes of a pen,
And of a beauty all in formulas.

I am ashamed of lying to my work,
And that my work should lie unto my life,
And of being able to accommodate myself,
While burning aromatics,
And of the musty odour reigning here. . . .

.   .   .   .

Water stagnating, in a pool's dark belly pent,
Water which greens at the soiled heart of old fountains,
Hides in its breast a life intense,
Quivers with being populous with beasts,
And with the long and languid dream of grasses;
It feels the fermentation of the living mud
Whose rotting in slow bubbles it exhales;

But it is blind and does not know the sky,
For death has sheeted it with withered leaves :
It cannot see save what it harbours;

But mute this water is, and cannot sing,
Nor laugh nor murmur like the sea and rivers :
And to itself can only strain a long-drawn echo;

14

But it is dead, and cannot roam,
And cannot run and leap and glitter,
Caressing quays and boats,
And cannot go to the embrace of mills ;
And cannot contemplate save life in its own self.
It is inhabited by life and lives not,
Even as is inhabited by life and lives not,
The inert life of corpses. . . .

And I should like to make come out of me,
To make a poem with, my steps,
Taking or no my pen to witness,
Taking or no my fellow-men to witness,
And I should like . . .

The stagnant water, too, would like. . . .

AND YET.

No water has abiding dwelling-place
Within one feeble hollow of the earth,
Which with the sky is face to face.
Let the noon glow, and the wind blow,
Some little of it must escape,
A flake of cloud or pearls among the grass.

Let the sun fill the house-wall yonder,
And blue be on thy highest pane of glass,
And thy feet shall be naked and warm among the
    sands,
And with thine eyes the birds shall wander. . . .

AN INN.

IT is an inn there is
At the cross-roads of Chétives-Maisons,
In the land where it is always cold.

Two naked highroads cross.
They never saw the garnering of harvests,
They go beyond the sky-line, very far.
These are the cross-roads of Chétives-Maisons.

There are three cottages,
In the same corner cowering, all the three,
Two of them are uninhabited.

The third one is this inn with heart so sad !
They give you bitter cider and black bread,
Snow wets the weeping fire, the hostess is
A forlorn woman with a smile so sad.

Only the very thirsty drink in it,
Only the very weary there will sit.
And never more than one or two together,
And no one needs to tell his story there.

And he who enters there with chattering teeth,
Sits down without a sound on the bench's edge,
Stretches his chin a little forward,
And lays his hands flat on the table.
One cannot think that there is flesh
In his stiff, heavy clogs;
His sleeves are short, and show
His wrists whose bone makes a red bowl ;
And he has eyes like a beaten beast's,
And obstinately stares at empty space.

He eats his bread with leisure,
Because his teeth are worn;
He cannot drink with pleasure,
Because his throat is full of pain.

When he has finished,
He hesitates, then timidly
Goes to sit, a little while,
At the fireside.

His cracked hands marry
The hard embossments of his knees.
His head inclines and drags his neck,
His eyes are ever scared at empty space.

His grief begins to dream, to dream,
And weighs upon his nape and eye-lashes,
And one by one makes wrinkles on his face,
While from the fire comes delicately clear
A new-born baby's weeping, far away.

And now a little girl he had not seen,
Comes from the corner where she sat;
A delicate and pretty little girl.

She has a woman's eyes,
Eyes widened suddenly with tears.

And now she comes anear him, very gently,
And comes to lean upon the stranger's hand
The tender flesh of her mouth;
And lifts to him her tear-filled eyes,
And reaches him, with all her delicate body,
A little flower of winter which she has.

And now the man sobs, sobs,
Holding in awkward hands
The little maiden's hand and flower.

. . . . . .

The forlorn woman with the smile so sad,
Who has been dumb and watching this,
Begins, as though she dreamed, to speak,
Begins to speak with far-departed eyes:

" A man came here who was not one of us . . .
He was not old with poverty and pain, as we are,
He was as sons of queens may be, perhaps,
And yet how like he seemed to one of us!
And no man ever spoke to me as he did,
Although he only asked to sit and drink;
He leaned his elbows on the middle of the table,
And all the time he stayed I looked at him;

And when he rose, I could not help but cry,
He was so like the one I loved when I was sixteen
      years . . .

He was opening the door,
To go back into the wind,
But when I told him why
The tears were in my eyes,
He shut the door again.

And all that evening, all that night,
His eyes and voice caressed me,
My folded pains, he stretched them out,

And spite of his young years and of my chilly bed,
Spite of my empty breasts and hollow shoulders,
He stayed a whole day long to love me, yes, he loved
    me . . .

And then this little girl was born
Of the alms of love he gave me . . ."

AFTER MIDNIGHT.

IT is at morning twilight they expire ;
Death takes in hand, when midnight sounds,
Millions of bodies in their beds,
And scarcely anybody thinks of it . . .

O men and women, you
About to die at break of day,
I see your hands' uneasy multitude,
Which now the blood deserts for ever !

White people in the throes of death,
Wrestling in all the world to-night,
And whom the weeping dawn will silence,
Fearful I hear your gasping breath !

How many of you there are dying !
How can so many other folks be lying
Asleep upon the shore of your death-rattles !

. . . Here is noise in the house ;
I am not the only one who hears you :
Someone has stepped about a room,
Someone has risen to watch over you . . .

But no !   It is a little song I hear.
If someone stepped about a room,
It was to go and rock a little child,
Who has been born this evening in the house.

INVECTIVE.

MAN whom I work for, I am angry with you ;
But not because you pay me to possess
My loveliest day of days, my dearest hours,
And for the right of fixing to your things my eyes ;

I am not angry with you for the sake of light
Dancing elsewhere, upon the river and on flowers,
Nor for the sake of what my thought leaves other-
    where,
Nor even for my independence gone.

No, but because you have not made me love you and
    esteem you,
For all the hope I had of it
And my good-will . . .

No, but because instead of joy,
You make me know
The ugliness of earning my own bread,
Yea, and the grief of helping one I scorn.

Yet I was very eager to absolve you,
If I could only find that you
Loved just a very little for itself
'The task you give my hands and yours to do ;

Had you been just a little like the farmer
Who does not need, to live in happiness among his
  beasts,
To calculate the money of their flesh and wool ;
If I had only found
That you, in short, had some faith in the part you
  play,
Whate'er it was, then I had given to you in full
The reverence which is due to any beauty,
Then I had seen your words illuminated
By fire enough for joy and zest of duty.

But no, your actions showed me plain
That my toil, and your care and calculating
Had for their only aim your vulgar pelf ;

And that my hands were your accomplices
And that my eyes were witnesses !

LANDSCAPE.

THIS was indeed a spot where sickly earth
Was poorly clad ;
Roads strewn with slag, and gathered stones,
And nettle-blinded puddles.

Over a rubbish heap
There was a scraggy path,
For ever sick of being perched so steep,
Without communion with the earth :
The shrubs that had been planted on it
Were dead already all along one side.

You saw, besides, a little rolling-mill,
Low and dilapidated in lucerne,
Whose chimney, with spasmodic jerks,
Spat at the sky its dry and hollow puffs.

Spite of chaotic glaciers of clouds,
Rearing around an amicable blue,
It was a wretched landscape, truly.

And yet you found there, if you looked,
A good place of green grass,
And yet of listening ears there could be heard
A noise of foliage,
And of pursuing birds . . .

Yea, if one had enough of love,
The wind might be petitioned, even there,
For music and for fragrance ;
And even there the forest could be found,
And sunshine playing in the verdure,
And hurtling on the stones with violence :
And, even there, a man might find quite near him
Arid and savage plains,
And fields in ecstasy.

And even thence a man might take
A recollection of the opulent earth,
A tufted memory rich as any garland,
As durable as songs of childhood are,
And penetrating as an echo is.

BIBLIOGRAPHY.

Books from which poems have been translated or quoted. Publication at Paris, unless otherwise mentioned. Mercure = Mercure de France.

Arcos (René), Ce qui naît, Figuière, 1911.
Barbusse (Henri), *Couturière*, poem included in Poètes d'aujourd' hui (see "Anthologies").
Bataille (Henri), Le beau Voyage, Fasquelle, 1904.
Berrichon (Paterne), Poèmes décadents 1883-95, Messein, 1910.
Duhamel (Georges), Selon ma Loi, Figuière, 1910.
—— Le Masque, Brussels, Nos. 6 and 7, Oct.-Nov., 1910.
Fort (Paul), Ballades françaises, 8 vols., Mercure, since 1896.
Gourmont (Remy de), Simone, Mercure, 1901.
Gregh (Fernand), La Maison de l'Enfance, Calman-Lévy, 1897.
—— La Beauté de vivre, Calman-Lévy, 1900.
—— Les Clartés humaines, Fasquelle, 1904.
—— La Chaîne éternelle, Fasquelle, 1910.
Guérin (Charles), Le Sang des Crépuscules, Mercure, 1895.
—— Le Cœur solitaire, Mercure, 1898. (Revised ed., Mercure, 1904.)
—— Le Semeur de Cendres 1898-1900, Mercure, 1901.
Herold (A.-Ferdinand), Au Hasard des Chemins, Mercure, 1900.
Humières (Robert de), Du Désir aux Destinées, Mercure, 1902.
Jammes (Francis), De l'Angelus de l'Aube à l'Angelus du Soir, 1889-97, Mercure, 1898.
—— Le Deuil des Primevères, Mercure, 1901.
—— L'Eglise habillée de Feuilles, Mercure, 1906.
—— Clairières dans le Ciel, Mercure, 1906.
Kahn (Gustave), Premiers Poèmes, Mercure, 1897.

Klingsor (Tristan), Schéhérazade, Mercure, 1903.
—— Le Valet de Cœur, Mercure, 1908.
Laforgue (Jules), Poésies, Mercure, 1903.
Lahor (Jean), Œuvres choisies de, Librairie des Annales [1909].
Lièvre (Pierre), Jeux de Mots, P. V. Stock, 1909.
Mallarmé (Stéphane), Vers et Prose, Perrin, 1908.
Mauclair (Camille), Sonatines d'Automne, Perrin, 1894.
Merrill (Stuart), Poèmes, 1887-97, Mercure 1897.
—— Les quatre Saisons, Mercure, 1900.
—— Une Voix dans la Foule, Mercure, 1909.
Moréas (Jean), Premières Poésies, 1883-86, Mercure, 1907.
—— Poèmes et Sylves, 1886-96, Mercure, 1907.
Mortier (Alfred), Le Temple sans Idoles, Mercure, 1909.
Nau (John Antoine), Hiers bleus, Messein, 1904.
Noailles (Countess Mathieu de), Le Cœur innombrable
    Calman-Lévy, 1901.
—— L'Ombre des Jours, Calman-Levy, 1902.
—— Les Éblouissements, Calman-Lévy, 1907.
Picard (Hélène), L'Instant Éternel, Sansot et Cie, 1907.
—— Les Fresques, Sansot, 1908.
Quillard (Pierre), La Lyre héroïque et dolente, Mercure, 1897.
Raynaud (Ernest), La Couronne des Jours, Mercure, 1905. ·
Régnier (Henri de), Premiers Poèmes, Mercure, 1899.
—— Poèmes, 1887-92, Mercure, 1895.
—— Les Jeux rustiques et divins, Mercure, 1897.
Retté (Adolphe), Œuvres complètes, Poésies, 1887-92, Biblio-
    thèque artistique et littéraire, 1898.
Rimbaud (Jean-Arthur), Œuvres de, Mercure, 1898.
Roinard (Paul-Napoleon), La Mort du Rêve, Mercure, 1902.
Romains (Jules), La Vie Unanime, Editions de L'Abbaye, 1908.
—— Un Etre en Marche, Mercure, 1910.
—— Deux Poèmes, Mercure, 1910.
Samain (Albert), Au Jardin de l'Infante, Mercure, 1893.
—— Aux Flancs du Vase, Mercure, 1898.
Souza (Robert de), Les Graines d'un Jour, Floury, 1901.
Spire (André), Versets, Mercure, 1908.
—— Vers les Routes absurdes, Mercure, 1911.
Thomas (Louis), Les douze Livres pour Lily, les Bibliophiles
    fantaisistes, 1909.
Verlaine (Paul), Choix de Poésies, Fasquelle, 1891.
Vielé-Griffin (Francis), Poèmes et Poésies, Mercure, 1895.
—— La Clarté de Vie, Mercure, 1897.
—— Plus loin, Mercure, 1906.
Vildrac (Charles), Images et Mirages, "L'Abbaye, 1908.
—— Livre d'Amour, Figuière, 1910.

Anthologies.

Bever (Ad. van) and Léautaud (Paul), Poètes d'Aujourd'hui, 2 vols., Mercure, 18th edit., 1908.
Séché (Alphonse), Les plus jolis vers de l'Année, 1907.08-09-10, Louis Michaud.
—— Les Muses françaises, Anthologie des Femmes-Poètes, vol. ii., xxᵉ. siècle, Michaud.

Literature (selected).

Babbitt (Irving), The New Laokoon, An Essay on the Confusion of the Arts, London, Boston, and New York, 1910.
Beaunier (André), La Poésie nouvelle, Mercure, 1902.
—— La Littérature française contemporaine, *Nineteenth Century and After*, Jan., 1910.
Berrichon (Paterne), Vie de J. A. Rimbaud, Mercure, 1897.
Bocquet (Léon), Albert Samain, sa Vie, son Œuvre, Mercure, 1905.
Brandes (Georg), Samlede Skrifter, vol. vii., Copenhagen, 1901.
Braun (Thomas), Des Poètes simples : Francis Jammes, Brussels, féd. de la libre Esthétique, 1900.
Delior (Paul), Remy de Gourmont et son Œuvre, Mercure.
Duhamel (Georges), et Vildrac (Charles), Notes sur la Technique poètique, Figuière, 1910.
Gide (André), Prétextes, Mercure.
Gosse (Edmund), Questions at Issue, Heinemann, 1893.
—— French Profiles, 1905.
Gourmont (Jean de), Jean Moréas, Sansot, 1905.
—— Henri de Régnier et son œuvre, Mercure, 1908.
—— Muses d'aujourd'hui, Mercure, 1910.
Gourmont (Remy de), Le Livre des Masques, 2 vols., Mercure, 1896 and 1898.
—— Promenades littéraires, 2 vols., Mercure, 1895 and 1896.
Grierson (Francis), Parisian Portraits, Stephen Swift, 1911.
Hamel (A. G. van), Het Letterkundig Leven van Frankrijk, Amsterdam, Kampen & Zoon [1907].
Hauser (Otto), Weltgeschichte der Literatur, 2 vols., Bibliographisches Institut, Leipzig and Vienna, 1910.
Huret (Jules), Enquête sur d'évolution littéraire, Charpentier, 1891.
Kahn (Gustave), preface to Premiers Poèmes, Mercure, 1897.
—— Symbolistes et Décadents, Mercure, 1902.

Landry (Eugène), La Théorie du rythme, et le rythme du français déclamé, Champion, 1911.

Leautaud (Paul), Henri de Régnier, Sansot et Cie, 1904.

Lièvre (Pierre), Notes et Reflexions sur l'Art poétique, Grasset, 1911.

Maassen (Henry), La Poésie paroxyste : Nicolas Beauduin Liège, éditions de la Sauterelle verte [? 1910].

Mauclair (Camille), Jules Laforgue, Mercure, 1896.

Mockel (Albert), Propos de Littérature, Mercure, 1894.

—— Stéphane Mallarmé : Un Héros, Mercure, 1899.

—— La Littérature des Images, *La Wallonie*, 20th Dec., 1887.

Moore (Goorge), Impressions and Opinions. Two unknown Poets, Walter Scott, 1891.

Pilon (Edmond), Francis Jammes et le Sentiment de la Nature, Mercure, 1903.

Querlon (P. de), Remy de Gourmont, Sansot, 1903.

Retté (Adolphe), Le Symbolisme, Messein, 1903.

Rimbaud (Jean-A.), Lettres de, Mercure, 1899.

Souza (Robert de), La Poésie populaire et le Lyrisme senti-mental, Mercure, 1899.

Symons (Arthur), The Symbolist Movement in Literature, Heinemann, 1899.

Thompson (Vance), French Portraits, Boston, 1900.

Viollis (Jean), Charles Guérin, Mercure, 1909.

Visan (Tancrède de), L'Attitude du Lyrisme contemporain, Mercure, 1911.

Yeats (W. B.), The Symbolism of Poetry, vol. vi. of Collected Works, 1908.

Zweig (Stefan), Paul Verlaine, vol. xxx. of Die Dichtung, Schuster & Loeffler, Berlin.

NOTES.

Page xvi ff.—A history of the symbolist movement is badly needed. A.-F. Herold's lectures on the subject (*Histoire de la Poésie symboliste*), 1906-1907, do not seem to have been published. The best sketch of the origins seems to me to be the Dutch essay, *Fransche Symbolisten*, by A. G. van Hamel (*Het Letterkundig Leven van Frank-rijk*). He gives the following dates :

According to Gustave Kahn the symbolist movement began in 1878-79, when Gustave Kahn, then twenty years old, was running about with vague plans for the renovation of French poetry in his head, and with samples of "rhythmic prose" in his portfolio. In 1880 Kahn became acquainted with Laforgue, and the two friends discussed "free verse" and "the philosophy of the unconscious." Kahn had then to fulfil his period of military service, and was for four years in Algeria, out of touch with literary life in Paris, except for his correspondence with Laforgue. When he returned to Paris in the autumn of 1885 he found much that was changed. Not that the traditional form of French verse had lost much prestige, though Verlaine in *Jadis et Naguère* had allowed himself some freedom in the choice of rhythms and rimes ; but the star of Mallarmé was in the ascendant. On the 6th April 1883 the first number of *Lutèce* had appeared. In 1884 Verlaine changed his publisher ; his works had previously been published by Lemerre, the publisher of the Parnassians ; from this date his books were published by Léon Vanier (successor, Messein), who became the general publisher of the symbolists. In 1884 Jean Moréas published his first book, *Les Syrtes*.

The new style became notorious in 1885. In this year Vanier published *Les Déliquescences, poèmes décadents d'Adoré Floupette, avec sa vie par Marius Tapora, pharmacien de 2e classe* (title-page at "*Byzance, chez Lion Vanné*"). It became known later that this parody, which many people took to be serious, had been written by Gabriel Vicaire and Henri Beauclair. "Adoré Floupette," so ran the tale, was a member of the cénacle "Le panier fleuri," and a disciple of the "grands initiateurs de la poésie de l'avenir" "Etienne Arsenal" (Stéphane Mallarmé) and "Bleucoton" (Verlaine). "Décadent," said the public, taking their cue from such lines as

> " C'était une danse
> De la décadence,
>
> Comme un menuet
> Dolemment fluet.
>
> C'était des chloroses
> Et c'était des roses,"

and from such confessions as this:

> " Etre gâteux, c'est toute une philosophie,
> Nos nerfs et notre sang ne valent pas deux sous,
> Notre cervelle, au vent d'Eté, se liquéfie."

Gautier had called Baudelaire a "poète de décadence," and compared him with the Latin poets of the Roman decadence. Verlaine had written a sonnet beginning: "Je suis l'Empire à la fin de la décadence, qui regarde passer les grands Barbares blancs." In the *xixe Siécle* for 11th August, 1885, appeared an article by Moréas rejecting the term "decadent," and suggesting "symbolist." But others accepted "decadent," and on the 10th April, 1886, appeared the first number of Anatole Baju's magazine *Décadent*. In Baju's pamphlet, *L'Ecole Décadente* (Vanier, 1887), the decadent is set up as a model citizen. On the 11th of April, 1886, appeared the first number of *La Vogue*; on the 1st of October in the same year that of *Le Symboliste*, and on the same day René Ghil's *La Décadence*. The *Revue Indépendante* became an organ of the new direction with the first number of its third series, November 1st, 1886.

On the 18th September, 1886, *Figaro* published a manifesto by Moréas entitled "Le Symbolisme." On the 26th September following, Anatole France criticized this manifesto in *Le Temps ;* Moréas answered him in *Le Symboliste* for the 7th October of the same year. (These articles of Moréas are reprinted in *Curiosités littéraires. Les premières Armes du Symbolisme,* Vanier, 1889.)

Page xvi.—Richard Whiting gave the English attitude in Chapters III. and IV. of *The Island :* . . . "he advanced to salute another distinguished author who had just done six months. This, I learned, was the chief of the Symbolist School, who had been 'put away' as the result of a truly heroic attempt to live down to his own books. . . . I well remember joining in a whip round to enable him to recite before a few of the right sort such of his own poems as did not absolutely need washing with a sponge . . . Cleanliness was his abnormal state . . . the best way to take him in his humour was to meet him in a sty . . . His writings had infinite pathos as a revelation of his mental states. Yet I should have thought they should have been kept in jars . . ., and carefully sealed down when the microscopists had done with them, and when the weather was warm." What resemblance has all that to austere thinkers like de Régnier and Vielé-Griffin ?

Page xviii, Note 2.—These equations of Saint-Pol-Roux remind one of the *kenningar* of decadent Icelandic poetry: wave-stallion = ship ; battle-fish = sword ; battle-geese = arrows ; corpse-dew = blood ; etc.

Page xviii, Note 3.—A. G. van Hamel (*op. cit.,* p. 31) seems to identify Jacques Plowert with Paul Adam.

Page xix ff.—Confusion of *genres :* see Mr. Percival Pollard's *Masks and Minstrels of Modern Germany* (Heinemann, 1911), p. 201.

Page xliii.—"The poet of joy." "L'essence du monde, la substance des êtres n'est pas l'intelligence, mais l'activité ou la volonté, comme s'exprimerait Schopenhauer. Mais contrairement à ce que pense ce dernier, cette activité, principe de tout, ne saurait s'exercer sans dégager de la joie, car à toute fonction en exercice s'attache un plaisir. . . . Même la douleur est bonne, car elle est encore une puissance d'être et se confond avec cette joie sacrée, latente, intuitive qui bande perpétuellement notre énergie au fond de notre âme." Tancrède de Visan, *L'Attitude du Lyrisme contemporain*, p. 35. See same book, pp. 135-138.

Page lv.—De Régnier is now an Academician.

Page lvi.—Guérin, however, used assonances in his earlier work.

Page lviii.—Another anarchist poet is Jehan Rictus (1876- —), who was brought up in London and Scotland. His most famous book is *Les Soliloques du Pauvre* (*Mercure*, 1895), written in the most horrible Parisian slang, which he brings Christ back to earth to understand. In intent the book is Christian ; but Christians will say that blasphemy can go no further.

Page lvii.—Since the Introduction to this book was written an excellent appreciation of Remy de Gourmont by Mr. Arthur Ransome has appeared in the *Fortnightly Review* (September 1911).

Page lxxx.—"Unanism," as the doctrine of the Abbey School is called, derives, like "Futurism," from Verhaeren. The latest shoot from that mighty stem is the "paroxyst" school. Organ : *Les Rubriques nouvelles*, Paris. "Art dynamique que la philosophie bergsonienne non seulement justifie mais impose," says Nicolas Beauduin, trumpeter-in-chief, who has just published *Les Cités du Verbe*. There is something in Beauduin's theory of *exaltation : "*Au lieu de viser à susciter en nous la représentation d'objets déterminés, la poésie doit donc tendre idéalement à nous donner l'approximation paroxystique d'un absolu."

A play by Duhamel, *La Lumière*, was staged by the Odéon in April this year. It is published by Figuière. *L'Armée dans la Ville*, by Jules Romains, had gone over the same boards a month before; published by the Mercure de France. Romains has also published this year with Figuière *Mort de Quelqu'un*, a most remarkable novel.

Page lxxxii.—Gojon. The theme is topical. In *l'Illustration* for the 29th July, 1911, Rostand published *Cantique de l'Aile*—a poem which reaches such sublime heights as this:

> "Gloire à celui qui part
> Et puis que plus jamais on ne voit reparaître !
> Nul ne l'a rapporté,
> Nul ne l'a vu descendre. Ah! c'est qu'il est, peut-être,
> Monté, monté, monté."

Page 194.—"As on Good Fridays." In France, on Good Friday, the bells are believed to have left their spires to fly to Rome, whence they come back on Easter Monday.

THE WALTER SCOTT PUBLISHING CO., LTD.,

FELLING-ON-TYNE.

THE CANTERBURY POETS.

1/- VOLS., SQUARE 8VO.   PHOTOGRAVURE EDITION, 2/-.

Christian Year.
Coleridge.
Longfellow.
Campbell.
Shelley.
Wordsworth.
Blake.
Whittier.
Poe.
Chatterton.
Burns. Poems.
Burns. Songs.
Marlowe.
Keats.
Herbert.
Victor Hugo.
Cowper.
Shakespeare: Songs, etc.
Emerson.
Sonnets of this Century.
Whitman.
Scott. Marmion, etc.
Scott. Lady of the Lake, etc.
Praed.
Hogg.
Goldsmith.
Mackay's Love Letters.
Spenser.
Children of the Poets.
Ben Jonson.
Byron (2 Vols.).
Sonnets of Europe.
Allan Ramsay.
Sydney Dobell.
Pope.
Heine.
Beaumont and Fletcher.
Bowles, Lamb, etc.
Sea Music.
Early English Poetry.
Herrick.
Ballades and Rondeaus.
Irish Minstrelsy.
Milton's Paradise Lost.
Jacobite Ballads.
Australian Ballads.
Moore's Poems.
Border Ballads.
Song-Tide.

Paradise Regained.
Crabbe.
Dora Greenwell.
Goethe's Faust.
American Sonnets.
Landor's Poems.
Greek Anthology
Hunt and Hood.
Humorous Poems.
Lytton's Plays.
Great Odes.
Owen Meredith's Poems.
Imitation of Christ.
Painter-Poets.
Women-Poets.
Love Lyrics.
American Humor. Verse.
Scottish Minor Poets
Cavalier Lyrists.
German Ballads.
Songs of Beranger.
Poems by Roden Noel.
Songs of Freedom.
Canadian Poems.
Contemporary Scottish
    Verse.
Poems of Nature.
Cradle Songs.
Poetry of Sport.
Matthew Arnold.
The Bothie (Clough).
Browning's Poems, Vol. 1
    Pippa Passes, etc.
Browning's Poems, Vol. 2.
    A Blot in the 'Scutcheon, etc.
Browning's Poems, Vol. 3.
    Dramatic Lyrics.
Mackay's Lover's Missal.
Henry Kirke White.
Lyra Nicotiana.
Aurora Leigh.
Naval Songs
Tennyson's Poems, Vol. 1.
    In Memoriam, Maud, etc.
Tennyson's Poems, Vol. 2.
    The Princess, etc.
War Songs.
James Thomson.
Alexander Smith.

More's Utopia.
Sadi's Gulistan.
English Folk Tales.
Northern Studies.
Famous Reviews.
Aristotle's Ethics.
Landor's Aspasia.
Tacitus.
Essays of Elia.
Balzac.
De Musset's Comedies.
Darwin's Coral-Reefs.
Sheridan's Plays.
Our Village.
Humphrey's Clock, &c.
Douglas Jerrold.
Rights of Woman.
Athenian Oracle.
Essays of Sainte-Beuve.
Selections from Plato.
Heine's Travel Sketches.
Maid of Orleans.
Sydney Smith.
The New Spirit.
Marvellous Adventures.
  (From the Morte d'Arthur.)
Helps's Essays.
Montaigne's Essays.
Luck of Barry Lyndon.
William Tell.
Carlyle's German Essays.
Lamb's Essays.
Wordsworth's Prose.
Leopardi's Dialogues.
Inspector-General (Gogol).
Bacon's Essays.
Prose of Milton.
Plato's Republic.
Passages from Froissart.
Prose of Coleridge.

Heine in Art and Letters.
Essays of De Quincey.
Vasari's Lives.
The Laocoon.
Plays of Maeterlinck.
Walton's Angler.
Lessing's Nathan the Wise
Renan's Essays.
Goethe's Maxims.
Schopenhauer's Essays.
Renan's Life of Jesus.
Confessions of St. Augustine.
Principles of Success in Literature (G. H. Lewes).
Walton's Lives.
Renan's Antichrist.
Orations of Cicero.
Reflections on the Revolution in France (Burke).
Letters of the Younger Pliny. 2 vols., 1st and 2nd Series.
Selected Thoughts of Blaise Pascal.
Scots Essayists.
Mill's Liberty.
Descartes's Discourse on Method, etc.
Kâlidâsa's Sakuntalâ, etc.
Newman's University Sketches.
Newman's Select Essays.
Renan's Marcus Aurelius.
Froude's Nemesis of Faith
Political Economy.
What is Art?
The Oxford Movement.
Hume's Political Essays.
Rydberg's Singoalla.
Petronius (Trimalchio's Banquet).
Senancour's Obermann.

THE WALTER SCOTT PUBLISHING CO., LTD.,
LONDON AND FELLING-ON-TYNE.

THE WORLD'S GREAT AUTHORS.
New Series of Critical Biographies.

GREAT WRITERS.

Cloth, Gilt Top, Price 1s. 6d.

ALREADY ISSUED—

LIFE OF LONGFELLOW. By Prof. E. S. ROBERTSON.

LIFE OF COLERIDGE. By HALL CAINE.

LIFE OF DICKENS. By FRANK T. MARZIALS.

LIFE OF D. G. ROSSETTI. By JOSEPH KNIGHT.

LIFE OF SAMUEL JOHNSON. By Col. F. GRANT.

LIFE OF DARWIN. By G. T. BETTANY.

CHARLOTTE BRONTE. By AUGUSTINE BIRRELL.

LIFE OF CARLYLE. By RICHARD GARNETT, LLD.

LIFE OF ADAM SMITH. By R. B. HALDANE, M.P.

LIFE OF KEATS. By W. M. ROSSETTI.

LIFE OF SHELLEY. By WILLIAM SHARP.

LIFE OF GOLDSMITH. By AUSTIN DOBSON.

LIFE OF SCOTT. By Professor YONGE.

LIFE OF BURNS. By Professor BLACKIE.

LIFE OF VICTOR HUGO. By FRANK T. MARZIALS.

LIFE OF EMERSON. By RICHARD GARNETT, LL.D.

LIFE OF GOETHE. By JAMES SIME.

LIFE OF CONGREVE. By EDMUND GOSSE.

LIFE OF BUNYAN. By Canon VENABLES.

LIFE OF CRABBE. By T. E. KEBBEL, M.A.

LIFE OF HEINE. By WILLIAM SHARP.

LIFE OF MILL. By W. L. COURTNEY.

LIFE OF SCHILLER. By H. W. NEVINSON.

LIFE OF CAPTAIN MARRYAT. By DAVID HANNAY.

LIFE OF LESSING. By T. W. ROLLESTON.

LIFE OF MILTON. By RICHARD GARNETT.

LIFE OF GEORGE ELIOT. By OSCAR BROWNING.

LIFE OF BALZAC. By FREDERICK WEDMORE.

LIFE OF JANE AUSTEN. By GOLDWIN SMITH.

LIFE OF BROWNING. By WILLIAM SHARP.

LIFE OF BYRON. By Hon. RODEN NOEL.

LIFE OF HAWTHORNE. By MONCURE CONWAY.

LIFF OF SCHOPENHAUER. By Professor WALLACE.

LIFE OF SHERIDAN. By LLOYD SANDERS.

LIFE OF THACKERAY. By HERMAN MERIVALE and FRANK T. MARZIALS.

LIFE OF CERVANTES. By H. E. WATTS.

LIFE OF VOLTAIRE. By FRANCIS ESPINASSE.

LIFE OF LEIGH HUNT. By COSMO MONKHOUSE.

LIFE OF WHITTIER. By W. J. LINTON.

LIFE OF RENAN. By FRANCIS ESPINASSE.

LIFE OF THOREAU. By H. S. SALT.

LIFE OF RUSKIN. By ASHMORE WINGATE.

Bibliography to each, by J. P. ANDERSON, British Museum.

LIBRARY EDITION OF "GREAT WRITERS."

Printed on large paper of extra quality, in handsome binding, Demy 8vo, price 2s. 6d. per volume.

NEW IDEAS ON BRIDGE. By ARCHIBALD DUNN, Jun.

INDIGESTION. By Dr. F. HERBERT ALDERSON.

ON CHOOSING A PIANO. By ALGERNON S. ROSE.

CONSUMPTION. By Dr. SICARD DE PLAUZOLES.

BUSINESS SUCCESS. By G. G. MILLAR.

PETROLEUM. By SYDNEY H. NORTH.

INFANT FEEDING. By a PHYSICIAN.

DAINTY DINNER TABLES, AND HOW TO DECORATE THEM. By Mrs. ALFRED PRAGA.

New Additions.

THE LUNGS IN HEALTH AND DISEASE. By Dr. PAUL NIEMEYER.

ALL ABOUT TROUT FISHING. By J. A. RIDDELL ("Border Rod").

HOW TO PRESERVE THE TEETH. By A DENTAL SURGEON.

1/- Booklets by Count Tolstoy.

Bound in White Grained Boards, with Gilt Lettering.

WHERE LOVE IS, THERE GOD IS ALSO.
THE TWO PILGRIMS.
WHAT MEN LIVE BY.   THE GODSON.
IF YOU NEGLECT THE FIRE, YOU DON'T PUT IT OUT.
WHAT SHALL IT PROFIT A MAN?

2/- Booklets by Count Tolstoy.

NEW EDITIONS, REVISED.

Small 12mo, Cloth, with Embossed Design on Cover, each containing Two Stories by Count Tolstoy, and Two Drawings by H. R. Millar. In Box, Price 2s. each.

Volume I. contains—
WHERE LOVE IS, THERE GOD IS ALSO.
THE GODSON.

Volume II. contains—
WHAT MEN LIVE BY.
WHAT SHALL IT PROFIT A MAN?

Volume III. contains—
THE TWO PILGRIMS.
IF YOU NEGLECT THE FIRE, YOU DON'T PUT IT OUT.

Volume IV. contains—
MASTER AND MAN.

Volume V. contains—
TOLSTOY'S PARABLES.

THE WALTER SCOTT PUBLISHING CO., LTD.,
LONDON AND FELLING-ON-TYNE.

Musicians' Wit, Humour, and Anecdote:

BEING

ON DITS OF COMPOSERS, SINGERS, AND INSTRUMENTALISTS OF ALL TIMES.

BY

FREDERICK J. CROWEST,

Author of " The Great Tone Poets," " The Story of British Music," Editor of " The Master Musicians" Series, etc., etc.

Profusely Illustrated with Quaint Drawings by J. P. DONNE.

In One Volume—Crown 8vo, Cloth, Richly Gilt, Price 3/6.

Among the hundreds of stories abounding in wit and pointed repartee which the volume contains, will be found anecdotes of famous musicians of all countries and periods.

THE WALTER SCOTT PUBLISHING COMPANY, LTD.,
LONDON AND FELLING-ON-TYNE.

14 DAY USE

RETURN TO DESK FROM WHICH BORROWED

LOAN DEPT.

This book is due on the last date stamped below, or
on the date to which renewed.

Renewed books are subject to immediate recall.

Lightning Source UK Ltd.
Milton Keynes UK
UKHW021439191118
332600UK00012B/1169/P